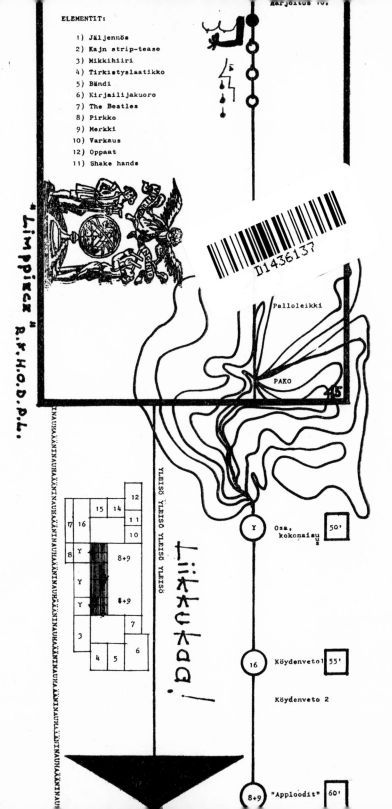

ELEMENTIT:

1) Jäljennös
2) Kajn strip-tease
3) Mikkihiiri
4) Tirkistyslaatikko
5) Bändi
6) Kirjailijakuoro
7) The Beatles
8) Pirkko
9) Merkki
10) Varkaus
12) Oppaat
11) Shake hands

"Limppixx" R.F.H.O.D.P.L.

Palloleikki

PAKO

45

YLEISÖ YLEISÖ YLEISÖ YLEISÖ

Liikkukaa!

12
15 14
17 16
11
10
8 Y
8+9
Y
Y
8+9
7
3
6
4 5

Y — Osa, kokonaisuus — 50'

16 — Köydenveto1 — 55'

Köydenveto 2

8+9 — "Apploodit" — 60'

The Music of Finland

Usko Meriläinen with his family, and their old English Sheepdog, Kuppe, outside their home in Tampere.

The Music of Finland

Denby Richards

HUGH EVELYN LONDON

For Inge and Henrik Antell

First published in 1968 by
Hugh Evelyn Limited,
9 Fitzroy Square, London W1
© 1968, Hugh Evelyn Limited
Printed in the Republic of
Ireland by Hely Thom Limited

Preface

ALTHOUGH I had been travelling the world fairly extensively over a period of some ten years, covering Music Festivals between Osaka in Japan and Stockholm, I had not been able to visit Helsinki before 1964. My reason for choosing that year was sheer selfishness. In 1965 Finland would be celebrating the centenary of the birth of Jean Sibelius, and I knew that I would be expected to attend the Sibelius Festival. Since I heartily dislike visiting a city for a major festival without knowing something of the atmosphere and the people, so essential to the spirit of the occasion, I decided to go the year before the Centenary, rightly assuming that 1964 would be a fairly quiet festival by comparison, and that this would give me the opportunity of getting to know both the Finns and Helsinki.

Accordingly, I arranged to visit the 1964 Sibelius Festival after the Danish Festival in Copenhagen. However, on arriving in Denmark, I found that Copenhagen had been chosen for the 1964 ISCM Festival, which ran currently with their own Festival, and I had to sit through a great deal of cerebral and emotionally cold modern music.

I have always regarded music as a means of communication through the senses, which pleases the intellect by its shape and form at the same time as the sounds themselves titivate our aural palate. Music which is primarily cerebral is as unsatisfying as music which is purely emotional sugar.

On arriving in Helsinki, I was met by Niki Vaskola, now one of the most enterprising members of Finnish Radio's music division, and then attached to the Festival, who offered me various musical events, including a concert of contemporary Finnish music in the Hall of Knights. After my experiences in

Copenhagen, I was in no mood for more modern fare, and it was only his extremely eloquent arguments which persuaded me to agree to go.

Perhaps it was the contrast between this music and the ultra-modern music I had heard so very recently that made the impact of this Finnish contemporary music so memorable, but I was as impressed by the individuality of the composers as I was by their obvious sincerity and ability to communicate.

Upon my return to England I wrote several articles on the subject, emphasising the fact that Finnish composers seemed to have recovered from the inevitable problem of being compared to Sibelius, and that they appeared to have kept up with many of the new musical idioms and ideas stemming from the rest of Europe, but, not being so immediately vulnerable as their counterparts in Germany and the other Scandinavian countries, they had had time to experiment and take what they felt best from these influences, rather than have to declare themselves as either disciples or 'squares'.

Since I was asked to write this book, I have had the chance to visit Finland on several occasions, to hear a considerable quantity of music and to become acquainted with many composers. What impresses me most about both the men and their music is their warmth and humanity; their insistence on artistic integrity and their uncompromising sincerity.

Realising that a book of this kind could do no more than speak of the composers and say something about their place in Finnish musical history, I felt that some effort should be made to have some of this music performed publicly outside Scandinavia. Accordingly, I suggested to Leonard Marcus, the founder and guiding spirit of past St. Pancras Festivals, and Councillor John Richardson, of the London Borough of Camden's Arts Committee, that the 1967 Camden Festival should include some Finnish music, and their enthusiasm and help resulted in performances of no less than nine contemporary Finnish works, including six premieres, four of which were commissioned by Camden and chosen through a competition organized for the purpose and judged by a non-Finnish jury of musicians and critics.

Even before their first performances, the three prize-winning chamber works, Rautavaara's Third String Quartet, Meriläinen's Second Piano Sonata and Segerstam's Song Cycle 'Three Leaves of Grass' were published by Josef Weinberger Limited in London, and thanks to the efficiency of Richard Toeman of their office, were on sale to the audience at the Festival performances.

Press reviews varied from luke-warm to enthusiastic, but the general impression was aptly summed up by Edward Greenfield in the *Guardian*, when he wrote that 'Anyone who may have the vague impression that Finnish music today is like Sibelius watered down will certainly have to think again after Camden.' Certainly the audiences were impressed, and gave the composers, who had been invited to England for the occasion, a great welcome.

This book, then, is intentionally more informative than erudite. It is written for the interested music-lover, to give him a background against which to listen to those of the Finnish works which are beginning to creep into international programmes. Many of the names mentioned will remain merely as names, but they have all had a part in creating a lively and intensely serious musical culture in a country which is becoming increasingly important in the fields of commerce and design.

I would like to thank all the composers and musicians in Finland who have given me so much of their time and friendship, and also the Music Division of Finnish Radio for the generous help I received in the task of hearing miles of taped music in their listening rooms. Both Kai Maasalo, the genial Head of Music and Niki Vaskola were invaluable and tireless friends during my Finnish visits, as were also Göran Stennius of the Ministry of Foreign Affairs and Ragnar Meinander of the Finnish Ministry of Education, without whom the co-operation with the Camden Festival would have been impossible. In London Henrik Antell and his efficient secretary Ritva Tiukkanen did more than any normal Cultural Attaché should be called upon to do, in dealing with my many requests and problems.

Thanks to the interest of Alex Saron of Philips Phonographic Industries in Holland, the works heard in London were recorded in June, 1967, by the same artists who had premiered them in Camden, and are available in Philips Modern Music Series for those who wish to hear some contemporary Finnish music at home. The numbers are 802854 L7 and 802855 L7.

My sincere appreciation to Brenda Dennis and Anne Williams for their help with the early drafts, to Wendy Moody for tackling the gargantuan task of typing the final script, and Marketta Benn for translating the many pages of Finnish information used in the appendix, where you will find as complete a list of contemporary Finnish works as I could wrest from the very shy and reluctant composers. Finally, my heartfelt thanks to Rhondda Gillespie for playing a great deal of piano music to me, and to Michael Reynolds for his help in putting my grammar in order!

LONDON, 18 June 1967.

I

THE AVERAGE Englishman is not too far wrong when he thinks, rather loosely, of Finland as a land of desolate wastes. The Finns call their country *Suomi*, sometimes derivated from the word *suo*, meaning swamp, and indeed, one third of the area consists of peaty marshes similar to the peat bogs of Ireland or the mosses of Lancashire.

Moreover, the general bleakness is further emphasised by the fact that two-thirds of the year is bitterly cold and when the Land of the Midnight Sun becomes the Land of the Mid-day Moon, short nights stretch into interminable day in this country which celebrated its first half century of independence in 1967, after more than a century as an autonomous Grand Duchy within the Tzarist Russian Empire, preceded by over 600 years as part of the Kingdom of Sweden.

It is only through the intense individualism of the Finn, that a national personality has survived, despite the intrusion of other cultures down the centuries, preserving intact and unbroken for the musical historian a distinct and traceable Finnish culture back to earliest times. As in the case of practically every western country, there are editions of songs, choral works and other primarily religious products dating from the Middle Ages. For example, the Turku Diocesan Liturgy established about 1330, incorporates several original features from religious festivals connected with local saints, particularly the patron of Finland, the English-born St. Henry. Again, as in practically every western country, this music is virtually never heard, except in such a case as the Finnish carol *Good King Wenceslas*—which few realise comes from Finland.

The comparative inaccessibility of Finland meant that instrumental music remained almost unheard during the seventeenth century when music and opera were flourishing throughout Europe. With no princely courts of its own, people had little chance to hear any other than music of their own folk culture.

The royal patrons of musical Europe had no counterparts in Suomi. It was not, in fact, until 1790 that Finland's first music society was founded in the former capital of Turku, but the Turku Music Society not only gave concerts, it also gave musical tuition, which was free to young people of limited means.

The sudden explosion of music at this time is demonstrated by the fact that between 1790 and 1808 the Society had 900 members, 70 of whom were active musicians, and possessed a library of some 2,000 scores, regarded at that time as the finest in the area that then comprised the kingdom of Sweden.

Most compositions heard in Finland and their performers were foreign until a few national composers began to emerge. Of these an important name is ERIK TULINDBERG (1761–1814), whose works included six string quartets and a violin concerto. Another Finnish composer, who succeeded in achieving some European fame during his lifetime, was BERNHARD HENRIK CRUSELL (1775–1838), who began his career as a military band player, becoming a clarinet virtuoso. Crusell lived most of his creative life in Stockholm, where his clarinet concertos are still occasionally performed.

In 1809 Finland was annexed by Russia and became a grand duchy of the Tsars but fortunately, cultural links with Sweden continued, operating simultaneously with the new link with Russia and its Asian culture.

2

In the 1820's, a music shop was opened in Turku, and for the first time an industry for the manufacture of instruments became established, until on 4 and 5 September, 1827, Turku was largely destroyed by a great fire. This caused the university to be transferred the following year to Helsinki, which not only became the capital, but also the centre of Finnish musical life.

In 1835, FREDRIK PACIUS (1809–1891), a German-born composer and violinist became professor of music at the university. Pacius, a pupil of Louis Spohr succeeded in raising considerably the standards of both teaching and music appreciation, and his importance in the musical history of Finland must not be underestimated. He happens, additionally, to be the composer of Finland's national anthem *Our Land*, to words by J. L. Runeberg.

RICHARD FALTIN (1835–1919), who succeeded Pacius at the university, came from Danzig. His contribution to the growing national music of Finland was exceptionally important in the field of church music. At that time, Finnish-born composers were completely unknown, even AKSEL GABRIEL INGELIUS (1822–1868), who was probably the composer of the first truly Finnish symphony, in which he made special use of the five-beat rhythm of the national rune melodies.

JOHAN FILIP VON SCHANTZ (1835–1865) was the first composer to deal with the Finnish epic poem, the Kalevala, in his *Kullervo* Overture, which is especially interesting since this particular tragic hero is also the subject of Sibelius' first major work.

Schantz's *Kullervo* Overture was written in 1860 for the opening of a new theatre in Helsinki, but it was obvious to those interested in music in Finland that no really important compositions were likely to be forthcoming until the background, and more particularly the creation of a first-class professional orchestra, would make conditions in which it would be possible for composers to have their works adequately performed.

The year 1882 saw the birth of Finnish musical life as it is today. In that year MARTIN WEGELIUS (1846–1906) founded the

Helsinki Institute of Music—now the Sibelius Academy. The story of his fight to establish a permanent home for musical education in Finland is a fascinating one, including the fact that this most extraordinary man went abroad to find young first-rate teachers, and that when he found that there were no text-books available, he sat down and wrote them himself.

The same year, ROBERT KAJANUS (1856–1933) founded a symphony orchestra, which in 1914 became the Helsinki City Symphony Orchestra, and is proud to be known as the oldest concert orchestra performing on a permanent professional basis in Northern Europe. Kajanus conducted without a break for half a century, and earned himself a permanent niche in the history of European music by his championship and definitive interpretations, including recordings of the works of his friend and contemporary, JEAN SIBELIUS (1865–1957).

II

FROM THE 1890's until the 1950's, the influence of Sibelius within Finland was that of a father-figure and national hero. Within his music we have the duality of East and West which is to be found within the country as a whole and in fact, is one of the most interesting aspects of both Finland and Finnish culture. Sibelius' musical output was a legacy not only to Finland but to the whole world. The great legacy which was exclusively to his native land was the result of his intense interest in fostering the musical characteristics and potential of young artists, both by personal help and encouragement and also by constructive enthusiasm in helping formulate a policy which would enable the music conservatoires to train young artists and teachers. As these young people spread the word throughout Finland, the number of musically appreciative listeners would gradually increase.

Within Finland today, there is a strong and lively interest both in playing and listening to music. As in many other countries, this is more predominant in the smaller cities, where the distractions of big city life are less felt. The emergence of this tremendous genius, from what had been for so long, comparatively, a musical desert, first acted as a spur to fellow Finnish musicians. Later, it was to have a reverse effect, because inevitably every new Finnish work for many years was unfavourably compared with the greater compositions of the master.

I am convinced that Sibelius himself, much as he loved publicity and appreciation, would have been the first to decry this treatment of other Finnish composers; but unfortunately, such is the way of the world, and several fine musicians were unjustly neglected and made self-consciously over-critical of their own works by the very existence of Sibelius.

Another factor is the extreme age to which Sibelius lived. When we take into consideration the fact that he died in 1957 in his 92nd year, we must also remember that he ceased creative activity in the late nineteen twenties, so that for the last three decades of his life he was in fact a living legend. At the same time, Sibelius became a nationally heroic figure, since his music so often characterized the independent spirit of Finland up to the time of the granting of Independence in 1917, and during the difficult years which culminated in the winter of 1939–40.

It will take another decade or two, aided by the masterly biography written by Erik Tawaststjerna, before we are able fully to understand the Sibelius of the post-war years. Personally, I felt nearer to understanding his very solitary genius when I visited Ainola, the house named after his wife, in which he spent his latter years.

To sit on the little balcony and look out across trees and over the lake with the sure knowledge that you can observe without being observed (a typically Finnish delight), is an unforgettable experience, which I hope many pilgrims in the future will be able to share. Composers, artists and writers from all over the world would visit Sibelius at Ainola, and his creative spirit would often influence their ideas or even more, often encourage younger men to strike off along their own paths.

Two of Sibelius' contemporaries, in each case about ten years his junior, have made minor names for themselves, and each are especially interesting in view of the fact that they show special characteristics typical of their birthplaces. ERKKI MELARTIN (1875–1937) came from the east of Finland and SELIM

6

Uuno Klami as a young man.

Uuno Klami

Leevi Madetoja with his wife.

Armas Järnefelt

Leevi Madetoja

Yrjö Kilpinen, one of the world's
greatest composers of Lieder

Robert Kajanus, champion of
Sibelius and Finnish music

PALMGREN (1878–1951) from the west. It is fascinating to note that each moved in an opposite direction from the other, as their careers progressed: Palmgren became a professor of composition in the United States, whilst Melartin spent many years studying theosophy in India, returning to Helsinki where he became the first teacher of composition, and later headed the Helsinki Conservatory of Music for twenty-five years.

Melartin's music is virtually unknown and is mainly lyrical and elegiac. He wrote eight symphonies of which two were left unfinished, but critical opinion places his songs and incidental theatre music higher than the large-scale works.

Melartin's early training was at the Helsinki Institute of Music under Martin Wegelius—whom he was to succeed—and later under ROBERT FUCHS in Vienna. Fuchs also taught Sibelius and LEEVI MADETOJA, about whom later. Whenever Melartin's name crops up in Finnish circles, he is spoken of with respect and affection, as being a highly cultivated and outstanding personality. To him, music was one of many civilized forms of life which, in his case also included painting and an outstanding appreciation for literature. Melartin was a fine teacher, and a whole generation of Finnish composers owe their individuality to his liberal attitude and his respect for their own very diverse contemporary ideas.

Probably Melartin's finest pupil was UUNO KLAMI (1900–1961). Both composers came from the district of Karelia, situated on the coast of the Gulf of Finland, near the post-war national frontier of the U.S.S.R. In the case of Klami, his creative imagination was largely stimulated by the sea and the many forms it took during the changing seasons. Having studied at the Helsinki Institute of Music, Klami went for a while to Paris, where his natural feel for orchestral colour was strengthened by a period of study under Ravel. His three symphonies and many symphonic poems are fascinating examples of how to use the orchestra as a virtuoso instrument.

Palmgren has often been compared to Grieg, and there is no

7

doubt that his piano works, particularly the Piano Sonata, Op 11, are strongly influenced by the Norwegian composer. On the other hand, there are other, perhaps stronger influences. Having studied at the same time as Melartin under Wegelius, Palmgren went on to Berlin and Weimar, where his training both as composer and pianist was revolutionised under Busoni. He made extensive tours throughout Europe and the United States, performing a great deal of his own music, which included five piano concertos, the best known of which, *The Stream*, is based on the course of the River Kokemäenjoki, similar in conception perhaps to Smetana's *Vltava*, but nothing like so dramatic or effective. Palmgren himself described the title as a symbol of life, and the concerto had the distinction of being performed in Berlin by Ignaz Friedman. Palmgren loved writing for the piano, and has been called the Chopin of the North, but although he undoubtedly appreciated Chopin's work, it was probably Schumann who became the greater influence. Schumann's work as a music critic interested Palmgren tremendously, and he incorporated many of Schumann's ideas into his own work as music critic of a leading Swedish-language newspaper in Finland.

In all probability, the works of these composers have fallen into obscurity where they will remain, except for the occasional centenary or special anniversary. Interesting though the works may be, none of them is of sufficient greatness to establish them in the repertoires of the world's orchestras or soloists. Nevertheless, the composers themselves are very important, if only because they were the pioneers with Sibelius, and at the same time the teachers of the generation of composers whose work is the main subject of this book. Without them and their contemporaries, the rapid growth of musical knowledge, appreciation and composition in Finland could never have been achieved. However, before we leave the deceased, two other composers of genius deserve special mention.

Oskar Merikanto

Selim Palmgren.

Jean and Ainola Sibelius.

Ahti Karjalainen

Tauno Fylkkänen

Väinö Pesola

Taneli Kuusisto

III

IN DECEMBER 1965 I had my first taste of a Finnish winter. Helsinki looked like a picture postcard without Father Christmas, the streets were covered in snow, the people were covered in furs, and the country itself seemed extra bright in the early morning, and depressingly dismal as soon as the sun set shortly after noon. Nevertheless, although the temperature was below freezing, the cold was not as intense or fierce as we know it in London.

During this visit, I flew north to the town of Oulu, which boasts that it is the home of the most northerly professional symphony orchestra in the world. Here the temperature was —37°C and I found to my astonishment that the rubber soles of my shoes stuck to the pavement and practically prevented me from walking. The air was extremely difficult to breathe, and although I had no actual feeling of discomfort through cold, after walking a hundred yards without a fur hat on, I became light-headed and had to force my steps back to the clammy warmth of my hotel. How any race of people could have decided to create a city in these conditions is beyond me, but the Finns are no ordinary race of people.

It is not surprising that LEEVI MADETOJA (1887–1947) having graduated in music in Oulu, left his native town for Helsinki and the wide world, and rarely, if ever, returned to it. Madetoja's

2

father appears to have been anxious to find a settled occupation outside of Oulu, for he became first mate on a windjammer and went to the United States, where he died while on the Mississippi, leaving his widow in straitened circumstances to bring up young Leevi and his brothers. The young Madetoja worked in Oulu as a street cleaner—a fact which is commemorated in the city by the circumstance that a street has now been named after him! He later became a lumberjack, while at the same time studying in the local grammar school. It was during this period that he suffered a haemorrhage, which with its threat of possible death, undoubtedly influenced his outlook on life. In 1906, Madetoja left Oulu for Helsinki where he enrolled simultaneously in the university and the Institute of Music. In only four years, he had obtained degrees in both Music and the Humanities. The Piano Trio composed for his diploma was largely influenced by his teacher, Jean Sibelius.

In 1910, he went to Paris where he was immediately accepted as a pupil by Vincent D'Indy. Unfortunately D'Indy fell ill almost immediately, so that the influence on Madetoja was not so much a matter of musical instruction, as imbibing the French way of life. Frequent trips into the countryside, the ease and freedom of the French people helped to broaden and perhaps to brighten the outlook of the rather gloomy young Finn, who, rather than finding another teacher to Vincent D'Indy, insisted on studying by himself, and being as receptive as possible to all outside influences, whether musical or human.

After Paris, Madetoja went to Berlin where he met and married L. Onerva, the Finnist poet, whose work became significant in her husband's vocal music.

Madetoja's symphonic output has been greatly overshadowed by the figure of Sibelius, but I feel that his three symphonies, and the symphonic poem *Kullervo*—yet another work inspired by this Kalevalan hero—may yet come into their own. Nevertheless, Madetoja has a special place in the history of Finnish music as the composer of the first two Finnish operas. *Pohjalaisia* (The Ostrobothnians) is regarded as the national opera of Finland. Written in 1924, this opera takes as its theme the struggle of the Ostrobothnians (Finns from the district of Ostrobothnia) against violent oppression, and successfully combines folk-music material with a very marked personal style. Madetoja really understood the personality of his native region, and the success of *Pohjalaisia* both in Finland and abroad, is due to his ingenious method of using folk melodies in conjunction with his own creative skill.

The other composer who is better known than Madetoja outside Finland, also made a speciality of vocal music, but in his case he devoted his creative output to lieder.

YRJÖ KILPINEN (1892–1959) is one of the great composers of lieder. After studying at the Helsinki Institute of Music, he went to Vienna under Heuberger from 1910 to 1911, and to Berlin in 1913 and 1914, where he studied with Taubmann and Paul Juon. Kilpinen produced over seven hundred songs, primarily to Finnish, Swedish and German texts, culminating in the *Kanteletar* cycle, which has its basis in folk poetry.

In physical appearance Kilpinen has been described as a ramrod, lion-maned, north Germanic Viking chieftain. His use of fourths and fifths in harmony and melody, his attachment to use naturally the pentatonic scale and church modes gives his work a special arctic clarity. Whenever possible, he would avoid harmonic thirds and strive towards spaciousness, for Kilpinen loved nothing better than the breath of clear mountain air on top of a fell. Kilpinen wrote his songs in extended cycles, perhaps consciously endeavouring to create musical portraits of the poets. Many of his cycles exceed those of Hugo Wolf in size, and are almost symphonic in their conception.

As he became older, Kilpinen became more and more affected by a love of mysticism, a subject which has a great appeal for a Finn, and his latter songs show a tremendous mystical influence. He is a great composer, whose output continues naturally from the line of romantic lieder begun by Schubert, and his importance in Finnish musical life should not be underestimated, for

Kilpinen's lieder has become not only an influence on young composers, especially SEPPO NUMMI (q.v.) but also an interpretative inspiration for the young Finnish singers who are now emerging upon the western musical scene.

IV

Two composers of lesser rank, but highly important in the
development of Finnish music, are ARMAS JÄRNEFELT (1869–
1958) and OSKAR MERIKANTO (1868–1924). Järnefelt joined the
Institute of Music in Helsinki during the time when Wegelius was
at its head, and he also studied law at Helsinki University. It was
not long, however, before his entire concentration was devoted to
music. He continued his studies under Becker in Berlin and
Massenet in Paris, eventually being appointed conductor of the
Magdeburg Opera and the City Theatre in Düsseldorf.

Järnefelt's first appointment in Finland was as conductor of the
Viipuri Orchestra, but real fame began in 1907 when he became
conductor of the Royal Stockholm Opera, where he earned the
honorary title of 'Court Conductor' which later became 'First
Court Conductor'.

Although Järnefelt's output as a composer is not very large—
partly due, maybe, to the very little time he had free from his
work as a conductor—his songs and cantatas are still played
regularly in Scandinavia. He was a great admirer of Wagner, and
earned himself the reputation of being an important interpreter
of Wagner's music dramas. His symphonic poem *Korsholma*
shows how much he was influenced by Wagner's scoring, and it
deserves to be heard outside Scandinavia, if only to show the

world the more serious musical side of the composer of the popular little *Praeludium* and *Berceuse*.

Merikanto originally intended to become a concert pianist, but in fact became one of Finland's greatest accompanists. His output as a composer is primarily vocal and includes some 150 songs and three operas of which *Pohjan Neiti* (*The Maid of Pohja*) was the first Finnish opera.

Merikanto also held the position of organist at the church of St. John, as well as being the first teacher of organ both at the Helsinki Precentor-Organist School and the Conservatoire. His many years in this capacity have borne fruit in the fine tradition of organ playing now to be found throughout Finland.

Whilst he was composing *Pohjan Neiti*, Merikanto's young son AARRE MERIKANTO (1893–1958) used to lie underneath the grand piano. He grew into a composer whose musical personality was the opposite of his father's. Whereas Oskar was essentially a romantic who enjoyed composing small-scale works, especially songs, Aarre favoured works on a large canvas, using stark harmonies and linear counterpoint. After only one term at the Helsinki Institute of Music, the young musician left Finland to enrol as a pupil of Max Reger in Leipzig. Reger's comprehensive knowledge of the techniques of composition, and especially his skill in the use of counterpoint, had a lasting effect on the young Finn.

When he left Leipzig he spent some years in Moscow, where the colour and excitement of Russian music became added to his already well developed sense of form and style. It is significant that Aarre Merikanto's personality should have found a common bond with the mystical Scriabin.

The influences of both Reger and Scriabin are to be found in Aarre Merikanto's opera *Juha*, composed in the early 1920's but not performed until 1958, when the Finnish Radio gave the world premiere as a tribute following his death. A public production did not come about until forty-one years after the opera's completion.

Juha is a setting of a Karelian novel by Juhani Aho, whose forest drama appealed to the young composer's imagination. Unfortunately, the Finnish musical world, practically cut off from the rest of Europe, was unable to take the younger Merikanto seriously, and the total lack of interest shown to his early works had a depressing effect. Having heard a tape of *Juha*, I am of the opinion that this music will soon be revived and appreciated in Finland. It has been favourably compared with the early operas of Leoš Janáček, and indeed the folk idiom is not dissimilar, although the orchestral scoring is nearer to that of Richard Strauss.

Another important influence, that of Schoenberg, soon became evident in Merikanto's work. In 1925 Aarre Merikanto received a prize from Schott, the music publishers, for his Concerto for violin, clarinet, horn and string Sextet, an atonal and uncompromising chamber work in which each of the nine instruments is given every opportunity to show their individual qualities as well as their effectiveness in ensemble.

He was appointed professor of Composition at the Sibelius Academy in 1951, and his final years saw the gradual acceptance of Aarre Merikanto as an important figure in Finnish musical life. Many of his works, which had been neglected or unperformed, were resurrected and presented by Finnish Radio, and it can be truthfully said that his influence remains strong at the present time, as we shall see when discussing his two most gifted pupils, EINOJUHANI RAUTAVAARA (b 1928) and USKO MERILÄINEN (b 1930).

V

AT THE time of the centenary of the birth of Sibelius in 1965 there were forty-eight living composers in Finland, all of whom had been born during his lifetime. Of these, thirty-one were born before 1920 and suffered more than a little from living their creative lives in the shadow of Sibelius' genius. Nevertheless, although the bulk of these composers have not produced internationally recognised masterpieces, their tenacity and creative abilities, as well as their work as teachers throughout the country have been instrumental in giving encouragement and example to the younger generation of Finnish composers.

A few words on some of these mainly choral composers is necessary as an introduction to the works now being composed by the young Finnish contemporary composers.

In a country where towns and villages are separated one from another both by great distances and—in winter—inaccessibility, it is not surprising that much of the musical life is centred around choirs, organ or piano very often being the only available instrument. The standard of choral singing throughout Finland is extremely high, similar to that found in Wales.

VÄINÖ PESOLA (b 1886) is one of Finland's principal choral conductors and composers. A student from the Helsinki Philharmonic Society's Orchestral School, he widened his musical education both in Budapest and Vienna. Within Finland, Pesola has directed many singing festivals, as well as composing many works for male and mixed choruses.

His output is not, however, confined to vocal music. His chamber music includes a String Quartet, and apart from various orchestral suites based on folk material from different parts of Finland, he has written three symphonies.

Another composer who has written numerous works for male, female and mixed choruses, as well as for solo voice, is LAURI IKONEN (1888–1966).

His music is essentially lyrical, and his melodies are devoid of complexity. The works I have heard—which include *Elämän Lahja* (*Gift of Life*) for chorus and orchestra, and the Piano Trio —are simple, sincere, straightforward music showing strongly the influence of Sibelius. Ikonen never left his native country and remained untouched by the many musical innovations which arose during his lifetime.

EINO LINNALA (b 1896) was a pupil of Erkki Melartin at the Sibelius Academy, after which he studied in Germany and Austria where he was a pupil of Arthur Willner in Vienna. He, too, has written numerous compositions for chorus, as well as songs and cantatas. His most individual work, however, is to be found in his two symphonies and orchestral works. His *Suomalainen Rapsodia* (*Finnish Rhapsody*), for example, is a well written, colourful work based on folk tunes and rhythms, often reminding the listener of Tchaikowsky's *Little Russian* Symphony.

ERNEST PINGOUD (1888–1942) and VÄINÖ RAITIO (1891–1945) are often spoken of together. However, Pingoud was more colourful and warm than his friend. Raitio was attracted to Scriabin and his work is marked by a similar feeling for colour. Both composers had works performed in the United States between the wars, but their names, unfortunately, have now dropped from the repertoire.

SULO SALONEN (b 1899) has devoted his life to polyphonic music. A fine organist who has taken part in several church music courses in Scandinavia, his output includes 40 motets, numerous cantatas, a *Requiem* and several compositions for his own instrument.

BENGT VON TÖRNE(1891-1967) has earned himself a considerable reputation outside Finland. A natural linguist, he endeared himself to the cultural circles of London, Paris and Rome. Von Törne was an æsthete who talked with knowledge and appreciation on every facet of art and cultural history.

Born in Helsinki, he entered the Institute of Music in 1910, studying musical theory and composition for six years with Erik Furuhjelm as his principal professor. For his diploma, in 1910, he wrote a Piano Quintet which he showed to Sibelius. Thus began an association between the great Finnish composer and the younger musician which was to continue until Sibelius' death in 1957.

It was well known in Finland that Sibelius never accepted private pupils. Nevertheless, he made a special exception in the case of Bengt von Törne, who studied orchestration with Sibelius during the winter of 1916–17. In 1937 Faber & Faber in London and Houghton Mifflin of Boston published a book by von Törne called *Sibelius, a Close-up. A Record of conversations*, which perpetuates many of Sibelius' comments to his young pupil. Since then, the book has been translated into Italian, Swedish and Finnish.

Also in 1937, Bengt von Törne was invited by the London University to give a series of lectures on the history of Comparative Art, that is to say, the development of painting as a parallel to the evolution of music throughout the Middle Ages and Renaissance to the baroque period.

An avid scholar, von Törne has been a regular visitor to the libraries of London, Paris, Rome, Madrid, Munich and many other cities, and his researches have culminated in the publication of a dozen books written in Swedish on the history of culture and art.

His most ambitious literary work, a study of the Spanish

Renaissance was published in Stockholm and Helsinki in 1961. In 1964 he was given the honorary degree of Doctor by Helsinki University.

His musical output includes six symphonies, the latest of which was completed in 1966, three sinfoniettas for a Mozart-size orchestra, ten symphonic poems, a piano concerto and several chamber works, the most important being his second Sonata for violin and piano, Op 42.

Bengt von Törne is one of the few Finnish composers to have his works widely played in Europe. Performances have been given in Paris, Monaco, Cannes and Luxembourg, and in 1943 he conducted a festival of his own works at Venice. His name is often seen in Finnish programmes where, for example, his Fifth Symphony, Op 67, completed in 1964, received one public and three radio performances in the 1965–66 season. This thirty-minute symphony is stimulating and engaging music permeated by a deep serenity.

Von Törne was less of a national than an international composer. His many years spent living, studying and teaching in the cultural centres of Europe have broadened his musical language. His early association with Sibelius, himself an avid traveller, undoubtedly laid the seeds of internationalism, which has given his more mature work such a special character.

VI

THE FIRST decade of the 20th century produced a goodly crop of potential composers, including HELVI LEIVISKÄ (b 1902), Finland's most important woman composer. She gained her diploma in composition at the Sibelius Academy, after which she received several grants enabling her to go to Vienna to study with Arthur Willner.

Her compositions include two symphonies, a piano concerto, several songs and chamber music. The Second Symphony, Op 27, was written in 1924. This work, which opens quietly with oboes, clarinets and bassoons and ends as quietly with solo violin and harp, is conventionally classical in style and shows a well controlled discipline in its organic growth. The climaxes are approached by dramatically stirring music, and while the symphony cannot be called 'modern' in the context of the orchestral repertoire of the 1960's, it is satisfying, well constructed music well worth the occasional airing.

Apart from her compositions, Helvi Leiviskä writes critical reviews for the independent evening newspaper, *Ilta-Sanomat*, and is in charge of the library at the Sibelius Academy.

OSSI ELOKAS (b 1904) graduated from the Turku Institute of Church Music to the Helsinki Conservatory. His speciality was choral conducting, in which field he has achieved some prominence. In 1942 he was appointed precentor at the Töölö Church in Helsinki.

Although he has written a Wedding March and an *In memoriam* for orchestra, most of his work consists of short pieces for piano and violin as well as songs, cantatas and other choral works.

In common with their opposite numbers in other countries, many Finnish composers earn a living as teachers, passing on to a new generation the knowledge and skills they have themselves learnt and acquired. Among these is LEO HÄRKÖNEN (b 1904) who holds the post of music lecturer at Teachers' College. He graduated from Helsinki University as well as gaining a diploma in composition at the Helsinki Conservatory, where he studied with Erkki Melartin. His compositions include two symphonies and two large-scale chamber works, as well as many songs and smaller pieces for solo piano.

In view of the fact that he studied under Bengt von Törne, NILS LERCHE (b 1905) could be described as a grand-pupil of Sibelius. However, he also studied under Bengt Carlson in Vienna emerging as a composer whose music is distinctive for its flowing lines—especially noticeable in his Piano Concerto and the ballet *The Princess and the Shepherds*. His other works include several symphonic poems including one with the fascinating title *SOS*!

Concertos for organ and orchestra are rare nowadays, and performers on this instrument will be interested to add TOIMI PENTTINEN's (b 1905) Organ Concerto to their repertoires. Penttinen studied at the Viipuri Institute of Church Music as well as the Sibelius Academy. His output also includes some orchestral suites, chamber and choral music. He is at present holding the position of director at the Regional Academy of Music in Kotka, a lively port regarded by its inhabitants as Finland's most cosmopolitan city owing to the large volume of overseas shipping. The remains of the old Russian fortress just outside the town of Kotka were destroyed by the Royal Navy during the Crimean War, and the town itself was founded in 1878. Sibelius is commemorated there by the green oasis of the Sibelius Park in which there is a sculpture of eagles by Jussi Mäntynen symbolising the town—the Finnish word for eagle is *kotka*.

Another composer who lives away from the principal Finnish cities is ARVO RÄIKKÖNEN (b 1906) who is in charge of music at the Teachers' College in the shipping and industrial centre of Rauma, one of the oldest towns in Finland. He too was a pupil of Erkki Melartin at the Sibelius Academy, where he also studied musicology with Ilmari Krohn. His works include several cantatas in which the sea is the dominant influence and a collection of children's songs as well as a ballet pantomime for children.

Orchestral experience obtained as a viola player initially in the orchestra of the Viipuri Friends of Music, where he first studied violin and composition, and later with the Helsinki City Symphony Orchestra, undoubtedly accounts for the skilful string writing which is found in the compositions of LAURI SAIKKOLA (b 1906). His music is cast in the classical mould and is tuneful, often romantic and makes pleasant listening. His large-scale works include concertos for violin, cello and piano and four symphonies.

Unfortunately, the only work by Saikkola which is relatively easy to hear is his *Musica per archi* which is available on one of the Fennica records issued by the Society of Finnish Composers. This piece is well written, but by its very nature cannot be truly representative of this composer. There are shades of Grieg and some influence of Bartók, but Fennica would have done better to have included his Wind Quintet.

Simplicity and a straightforward approach to composition are also found in the works of TOIVO ELOVAARA (b 1907), who apart from composing, is a secondary-school music teacher and a precentor-organist. He has written primarily for small ensembles including a Sinfonietta for string orchestra, some string quartets and other chamber works. Elovaara has composed incidental music for stage productions as well as songs and choral works.

Few musicians can claim to have played both violin and trombone in different orchestras, but this is the case with ARTI KARJALAINEN (b 1907), one of Finland's most versatile musicians. He studied composition at the Helsinki Conservatory and also at the Viipuri Institute of Music, later going to the Sibelius Academy where he stayed to teach and train the children's orchestra. From here, he moved to the town of Jyväskylä in central Finland, where he conducted the City Orchestra and taught at the local music institute. He has also conducted the Kotka City Orchestra before being appointed as municipal director of music in Jyväskylä.

In spite of a busy life as an active musician, Karjalainen has proved to be a prolific composer, his works including a symphony, concertos for violin, cello and trombone, as well as a suite for oboe and orchestra. He shows a natural feeling for orchestral tone colours and his scores are stimulating and imaginative.

A pupil of Leevi Madetoja who now teaches and conducts in Helsinki is KALERVO TUUKKANEN (b 1909). His output is on a larger scale than most of his contemporaries. The music is essentially lyrical rather than dramatic and includes five symphonies, two violin concertos, a one-act opera and several major works for chorus and orchestra, one of which, *The Bear Hunt*, a setting of a text by Aleksis Kivi, won a silver medal in the art competition at the London Olympic Games of 1948.

The viola section in Helsinki's City Symphony Orchestra contained another composer apart from Lauri Saikkola. This is ERKKI AALTONEN (b 1910) who studied at the Sibelius Academy.

Although Aaltonen's compositions include five string quartets and other chamber music, he has specialised in orchestral works including four symphonies, two piano concertos and an orchestral suite entitled *Hämeenlinna*—the name of the town where Sibelius was born.

VII

FIVE COMPOSERS who belong to the decade covered by the last
chapter have risen to positions of importance within the administrative and cultural life of Finland. Needless to say, the demands
made upon them by their official duties have inevitably curtailed
the time available for creative composition.

For example, MARTTI TURUNEN (b 1902) is executive director
of TEOSTO, an organization maintained to protect composers'
copyrights and collect royalties, and the central figure in contemporary Finnish choral life. For many years Turunen was conductor of the Helsinki University Male Choir—with whom he has
frequently toured Europe and North America—as well as being
for some time president of the Finnish League of Singers and
Musicians. Among his many other posts, he is treasurer of the
Finnish Society of Composers.

Turunen has composed a Canzonetta and Serenata for
orchestra and also some piano pieces, but the bulk of his creative
output is vocal. He has taken a special interest in the acoustic
problems of choral singing and the various techniques of setting
words to music.

The present musical director of Finland's National Theatre is
HEIKKI AALTOILA (b 1905)—another of Melartin's pupils. In
this capacity, he has composed incidental music to over sixty plays

Aarre Merikanto

Lauri Saikkola

Jouko Tolonen

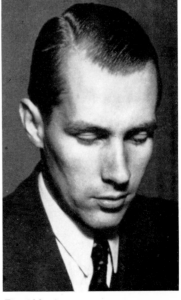
Einari Marvia

Kalervo Tuukkanen
Einojuhani Rautavaara

Usko Meriläinen

Joonas Kokkonen

Paavo Heininen

Tauno Marttinen

Leif Segerstam

Henrik Otto Donner with his wife

Reijo Jyrkiäinen

Aulis Sallinen

Erik Bergman

Henrik Otto Donner

including the *Merchant of Venice*, Thornton Wilder's *Our Town*, Tennessee Williams' *Cat on a Hot Tin Roof* and *A Streetcar Named Desire*, and Strindberg's *Fröken Julie*. In the cinematic field, Aaltoila has provided music to several dozen films. His other activities include the conductorship of many student orchestras, and also the post of music critic for the daily newspaper *Uusi Suomi*.

One of Helsinki's most important all-round musicians is TANELI KUUSISTO (b 1905) who is well known on the concert platform as a pianist as well as being a composer, the organist of the Töölö Church and rector of the Sibelius Academy. Needless to say, he has written many compositions for performance in church including a setting of Psalm 121. His song cycles include a tribute to one of Finland's best loved institutions, *Saunakamari* (*The Sauna Chamber*). In the orchestral field, he has written a symphonic poem and a Nocturne for cello and orchestra, as well as incidental music for films. Kuusisto is one of Finland's most cultured personalities, and is regularly being called upon to take an active part in the musical life of Finland, including the annual Sibelius Festivals.

The managing director of the Helsinki City Symphony Orchestra is NILS-ERIC RINGBOM (b 1907), a native of Turku, who took his Master of Arts degree there, specializing in musicology.

For several years, Ringbom was a violinist in the Turku Symphony Orchestra, after studying this instrument—as well as orchestration—with Leo Funtek. Ringbom, who is also a PhD in musicology, has been music critic of the *Nya Pressen* (formerly *Svenska Pressen*) since 1933.

His other activities include the chairmanship of the Finnish section of the ISCM and from 1951–60 he was artistic director of the annual Sibelius Festivals.

Ringbom was the first Finn to have a work chosen for performance at an ISCM festival. This was his Wind Sextet, which was played at the festival in Salzburg in 1952. He has also composed

25

several large-scale works including four symphonies, which represent his artistic development from 1938–62. The Third Symphony composed in 1948 opens with a rich cello theme, which sets the mood for a warm, expansive work. On the other hand, his Fourth Symphony, completed in 1962, is more astringent. Its three movements represent the Past, Present and Future: the first retrospective, the second short, rhythmically breathless and full of nervous vitality, whilst the third is a slow, inexorable, even pessimistic movement.

As a vocal composer, Ringbom has a natural understanding of the beauty of the human voice. In 1947 he completed his Four Songs for soprano and orchestra, which are simple, direct, evocative and poignantly beautiful.

One of the key pupils of Leevi Madetoja is OLAVI PESONEN (b 1909). His importance in Finnish musical life has resulted in his appointment as inspector-in-chief of musical education with the National Board of Schools. His early studies were at Helsinki University and the Sibelius Academy, and he also studied under Willner in Vienna.

As a composer, Pesonen has written two symphonies and other orchestral works, including a highly effective *Fuga fantastica*. His choral compositions demonstrate his great interest in Gregorian chant.

VIII

ERIK BERGMAN (b 1911) is not only one of the few really significant Finnish composers, he is also the first composer of international quality to be born in Finland after Sibelius.

Bergman's early years were spent studying at the Sibelius Academy, where he obtained his diploma in composition in 1928. He then went to Berlin to join Heinz Tiessen's master classes in composition, later going to Vienna where he became a pupil of Joseph Marx, but probably the greatest influence was that of Vladimir Vogel, with whom Bergman studied in Switzerland.

Bergman is an intellectual with a deeply rooted sense of logic. At the same time, however, there is a strongly passionate vein—sometimes warm sometimes white-hot—which holds the imagination as intensely as the logic of his composition satisfies our sense of form.

So far as the Finnish music world was concerned, Erik Bergman was regarded, until the early 1950's, as a fantastically successful choral trainer: his compositions were still moving towards maturity, whilst the composer himself was assimilating new colours and techniques from every possible source.

In 1953 came the *Rubaiyat*, a setting of part of Omar Khayyam's famous text for baritone, male choir and orchestra. This work immediately established him as a composer of importance who had freed himself from the tonal Sibelian influence which had dominated Finnish musical thought until that time. It broke new ground in its uncompromising use of percussion and the imaginative vocal writing. Hitherto, Bergman had been consciously experimenting, seeking his own musical language. Now, with *Rubaiyat*, he had entered a major phase in his development as a composer.

For the next five years he continued to explore instrumental and vocal tone colours. His *Exsultate* for organ, composed in 1954, made a considerable impact in Scandinavian musical circles for its imaginative treatment of the instrument, but even more impressive were his three vocal works, published under the single Opus number 47 and completed in 1958. The first, *Adagio* is for baritone, male choir, flute and vibraphone—an instrument which becomes increasingly significant in Bergman's compositions, whilst *Svanbild*—the second—is frequently performed separately.

Opus 48, *Aubade* was a milestone in Bergman's career. He had been invited to carry out research into the folk music of Turkey and Egypt and the colours, exotic atmosphere and a distinctively oriental flavour pervade this evocative orchestral tone poem. The work was performed at a meeting of the International Rostrum of Composers in Paris, where it was a tremendous success.

Aubade is an excellent work with which to make first acquaintance with Bergman's music. It is romantic, atmospheric and melodically fresh, each theme growing naturally from its predecessor and adding its own individual colour to the overall shape and logic of the work itself. Bergman's early experiments with all manner of instruments here reaches fruition both in his individual treatment of solo instrumental passages and the varied and imaginative ensembles. A large battery of percussion is used with discipline and imagination, but it is the underlying tension which really grips the listener and holds his attention. *Aubade* uses the serial technique of composition, yet this is of no more musical importance to the lay concert-goer than the fact that a Beethoven first movement is in sonata form. It is the music that matters—and it is the music which succeeds.

The following year, 1959, saw the composition of *Aton*, the background of which is rooted in the Egyptian Middle Empire. *Aton* is a setting of the Hymn to the Sun by the Pharaoh of the title, the poem being one of the oldest monotheistic works in literature. It is mystic, intensely religious and pervaded by the exotic atmosphere of a long distant and all but forgotten culture. The words of the poem are intoned by a speaker, while the solo baritone emphasizes and colours their meaning. A speaking chorus—firm evidence of Vogel's teaching—is used to heighten the atmosphere of mystery and vehemency by whispering effects, whilst the instrumental writing is on a large imaginative scale to convey the mobility and poignancy of the poem.

Bergman's work in pioneering a new vivid and exciting approach to choral music is the dominating factor in his creative output. Although orchestral pieces like *Aubade* and *Simbolo* (1960), together with his chamber works—the most important probably being the *Concertino da camera* for eight soloists, written for Francis Travis in 1961—have been recognized as important additions to the modern repertoire, it is the challenge and potential of the human voice which has fired Bergman's imagination.

I think that his greatest work is *Fåglarna (Birds)*, Op 56a, for baritone, male chorus, celeste and percussion, completed in 1962. This is a setting of a Swedish text by his wife, Solveig von Schoultz in which every device for producing atmosphere has been employed with the economical skill of a great craftsman, yet these devices, far from being an end in themselves, are merely tools used by a musician of genius to convey his musical intentions. There is a moment in *Fåglarna* when the choir create an impression of birds in flight by free repetition of the word *flykt*. This is at once the dramatic apex of the work and its *raison d'être*. *Fåglarna* is extremely complicated and can only be effectively performed after much intensive rehearsal. However, there is a recording issued in Finland to mark the 125th anniversary of the Akademiska Sangföreningen, Finland's principal male voice choir, in which Erik Bergman conducts *Fåglarna* as well as other Finnish choral music by Pacius, Palmgren, Sibelius and some of Bergman's contemporaries. This recording deserves to be better known—not only as an authentic performance of Bergman's work, but also as a practical demonstration of his eminence as a choral conductor and trainer.

Erik Bergman may well become a figure of historical importance for his pioneering of certain vocal and instrumental techniques, especially his experiments with speaking choir and with the delicacy of evocative scoring for percussion. Nevertheless, I am convinced that he will be recognized also as a giant among twentieth-century choral composers. He is not overprolific, but each new work is the end-product of much thought, deliberation and inner conflict. The inspiration, which starts the life-cycle of a new Bergman piece, comes generally during his all-too-short summer vacations in the country, where he can escape from the rigorous life of teaching composition at the Sibelius Academy, taking choral rehearsals with his two choirs, and conducting performances both on radio and in public, as well as the inevitable public calls upon his time.

In 1961 he was elected a member of the Royal Swedish Academy of Music, and in 1965 he was awarded the Wihuri Foundation International Sibelius Prize. His compositions are finding their way into the programmes of international music festivals and regular concert series in Europe and the United States. Bergman has much to say, and it may well be that his future works will gain more rapid acceptance throughout the world. However, it would be sad if *Aubade* and *Fåglarna* were to be neglected, as these two works alone are sufficient to establish him as a twentieth-century composer of the front rank.

IX

WHEREAS ECONOMY and ruthless pruning of all but the most necessary material is an important characteristic of all the works of Bergman, the strength as well as the weakness in the compositions of TAUNO MARTTINEN (b 1912) lies in his prolific, uninhibited spontaneity.

Marttinen has never been afraid to follow new paths, and he has been compared to Charles Ives for his pioneering and uncompromising approach to composition. His mind is always open to examine anything new and to grasp the musical implications of hitherto unexplored ideas. Once stimulated in this way, Marttinen cannot rest until he has put pen to paper and the ideas into practice. Without doubt, he is the most prolific of Finland's composers as well as one of the most individual.

In 1955, when he was in his forties, Marttinen came under the influence of Darmstadt. As a result he composed *Kokko, ilman lintu* (*The Eagle, Bird of the Air*) for mezzo and orchestra, which was awarded a special prize in the composition contest organized by the Cultural Fund of Finland in 1956.

Kokko makes free use of the twelve-tone system, and is a highly successful and evocative piece in which the poignant melody of the main theme rides delicately over a simple, finely drawn orchestral background.

Marttinen has composed major works for practically every musical medium including ballet, opera, film music and large-scale orchestral works. In the latter category, he has four symphonies to his credit. However, chiefly owing to his tendency to accept and use material as it flows from his fertile mind, the symphonies lack the discipline which is so necessary to the form.

On the other hand, Marttinen's Violin Concerto, composed in 1962, is one of his best works, as well as being a first-class addition to the repertory. The first movement is memorable for the uncompromising, strongly angular scoring beneath which the underlying musicianship and sincerity of the composer reaches out with stimulating vehemence. The second movement—Lento —has an inexorable pulse-beat on low piano, harp and tam-tam, over which the soloist discourses with growing melodic and harmonic intensity, rising to a great orchestral climax before gradually dying away to make room for a rousing finale.

All Marttinen's works show a partiality for dramatic use of percussion, whilst his scoring for oboe in melancholy or meditative moments is effective and moving.

In the last few years, Marttinen has established himself as an operatic composer. In this medium he was responsible for writing a one-act television opera based on Gogol's *The Overcoat*, which was produced by Finnish Television with tremendous success. I found the music rich and imaginative, but the production suffered somewhat by an over-stylized use of ballet sequences. Other operas by Marttinen include a setting of a Balzac story and *Apotti*, an opera buffa, one of the few effective works of this type written in this century.

Tauno Marttinen is at present the director of Hämeenlinna's Institute of Music, where he seems to find time to teach and compose as well, without losing the joys and stimulations of being head of a lively family. Although his contribution to Finland's musical life includes successful appearances as composer, conductor, pianist and lecturer, it is difficult to assess Marttinen's importance. He still has much to say, and maturity may well bring with it more self-discipline. There again, I think it very possible that Marttinen will distinguish himself in the operatic field where his fertile imagination and tremendous musicality will be able to work freely together. Whatever happens, he will always have an important place in Finland's musical history.

His Symphony No. 4 tied for the orchestral prize in the Camden Festival Competition in 1967.

X

AFTER A silence of six years, EINAR ENGLUND (b 1916) has returned to active composition with a Piano Nocturne, composed in 1966. It is to be hoped that this marks the beginning of a new phase in his creative life, for this composer has had a significant impact in Finland despite the fact that the Nocturne is only his fourteenth work. The Op 1 of this gifted pianist was a Piano Quintet (1941), but it was his next completed work—a symphony first heard in 1946—which immediately established him as a leading Finnish composer. This symphony is as much a musical record of the last war as Prokofiev's Fifth or Shostakovich's *Leningrad* Symphony. It is dramatic, pitiless and intensely moving: the work of a romantic composer whose intellectual capacities and tremendous interest in his fellow man shine through the pages.

The following year—1947—produced *Epinikia*, a symphonic poem for large orchestra which is organically powerful although the impact is not so searing as that in his First Symphony. The Second Symphony followed in 1948 and is as lyrical as its predecessor was angry. There is a slow movement evocative of a pastoral evening inspired by the contrast of a blackbird's serenade with the sounds of a warm summer night, which is one of the most beautiful expressions in all Finnish music.

It was not until he had composed incidental music to *The Great Wall of China*, a ballet suite, a film score and a cello concerto that Englund, already recognized in Finland as a pianist of stature, finally produced a piano concerto. This work is a product of a first-class pianist letting his hair down on behalf of his instrument. It is unashamedly romantic, virtuosi and effective. It is in fact a concerto in a tradition which has gone out of favour in our time, but nonetheless makes valid points, for all that.

His Introduction and Toccata, which was introduced outside Finland by the Australian pianist, Rhondda Gillespie, has proved to be a highly successful Finnish export. With its exciting cross rhythms, reminiscent of Falla, and its strong uncompromising sense of lyricism in the Introduction, this short recital piece may well become part of the standard repertoire of young pianists.

Englund has shown a special talent for writing music for the theatre. His *Odysseus*, completed in 1959, is regarded by some Finnish critics as the finest ballet music composed this century in Scandinavia. Perhaps this is the medium in which Englund will finally establish himself outside his native country.

Another composer of whom I am sure we will hear a great deal in the years to come is BENGT JOHANSSON (b 1914), an all-round musician who qualified at the Sibelius Academy in both composition and cello.

In common with Erik Bergman he has written works for speaking chorus, one of the most effective being a setting of *The Tomb at Akr Caar*. Since he is also an expert sound and electronic engineer, it is not surprising that electronic music has influenced and interested Johansson, although I found in *The Tomb* that the most stimulating moment was the use of the word 'soul'—the setting is of an English text by Ezra Pound—rather than the all too familiar electronic devices, which would be more at home as *Son et Lumière* accompaniment at some remote Egyptian tomb.

A piano concerto, some variations for cello and orchestra and a *Stabat Mater* for chorus are included in Bengt Johansson's list of compositions. However, he is regarded in Finland as one of the most interesting composers for chorus, and his present work as sound-recording expert to the Finnish Radio, especially respecting the recently formed, yet already established Finnish Radio Chamber Choir, should bear more and more fruit in the near future.

In 1967 he completed an impressive Requiem. This is really concentrated music, lasting just over half-an-hour, and scored for a huge orchestra and chorus with divisions, requiring more than one conductor

At its first performance in Helsinki, the work was hailed as a masterpiece. It could be argued that it is uneconomical but its length would allow for its inclusion in many major choral/orchestral concerts these days.

XI

OTHER COMPOSERS whose births occurred during the second decade of this century, have made special contributions to Finnish music. VILHO LUOLAJAN-MIKKOLA (b 1911), who teaches music in primary schools in Helsinki, studied theory and composition at the Sibelius Academy and also graduated at a teachers' college. His output concentrates on songs and choral works, with a strong folk element which is also to be found in some of his chamber works.

JOUKO TOLONEN (b 1912) is the composer of a symphony, songs and piano music. He has held the post of music supervisor of the Finnish Broadcasting Corporation as well as being manager of the Finnish National Opera.

Tolonen's music is conventional but extremely likeable. His *Andante and Rondo alla burla* is a 10-minute piece for full orchestra guaranteed to send any audience away happy and excited. It shows the sincere confident writing of a composer who feels the moods and emotions he expresses and knows how to transfer them into sound. He has a special rapport for the more doleful side of the clarinet which particularly appeals to me.

Originally AHTI SONNINEN (b 1914) was destined as a primary school teacher, but he studied music privately with Eino Linnala before entering the Sibelius Academy and it was not long before his individual exuberance asserted itself in composition. His *Symphonic Sketches* are a good example of Sonninen's infectious *joie de vivre* and have deservedly won critical praise away from Finland. He has a natural gift for orchestral colour in which the influences of Bartók and Shostakovich are heard; but their impact is swamped by his own rhythmic and harmonic ideas.

Sonninen's output includes concertos for violin and piano, several symphonic suites, numerous cantatas and a great deal of music for the theatre, of which the ballet score to *Pessi and Illusia*, based on a modern fairy-tale by Yrjö Kokko has attracted special attention.

It is impossible to visit Helsinki without noticing Fazer's impressive music store. EINARI MARVIA (b 1915) is the director of the publishing department. A pupil of Erkki Melartin at the Helsinki Conservatory, whilst at the same time studying law at the university, Marvia obtained a baccalaureate in the humanities. As a composer, he has been most effective as a song writer in which the dominant influence has been that of Yrjö Kilpinen. However Marvia has written two piano sonatas, also a quintet for woodwind and several orchestral works of which the most important is the symphonic poem *Taru* (*Legend*).

Another composer who spends much of his time in a music shop is ERIK FORDELL (b 1917). He is to be found in the head office of Soitin ja Radio, the principal music store in Kokkola. Fordell is a prolific composer with fourteen symphonies to his credit as well as a violin concerto, a piano concerto, a horn concerto and suites for both strings and full orchestra. He has also composed some 400 songs.

EERO SIPILÄ (b 1918) is a solitary figure from the north-eastern part of Finland, where he teaches music in the Teachers' College of Kajaani. In his relatively few compositions Sipilä makes frequent use of modern stylistic devices. One of the most colourful is *Super flumina Babylonis*, a setting of the 137th Psalm which has been performed in London by the Finnish Radio Chamber Choir. Sipilä ends this composition by building a huge cluster, starting from a pianissimo unison and raising the chord step by step to a great fortissimo.

Probably the most widely known operatic composer in Finland is TAUNO PYLKKÄNEN (b 1918) who began composing whilst still a child. In fact, his first opera *Bathseba Saarenmaalla* (*Bathsheba at Saarenmaa*), a one-act setting by Aino Kallas, was composed when he was twenty-two, the same year in which he gained his diploma at the Sibelius Academy and gave a highly successful concert of his works in Helsinki. Since that time, Pylkkänen has gone from strength to strength. In 1950, his opera *The Wolf's Bride* won the coveted Prix Italia.

His mother was a well known actress and his early proximity to the theatre undoubtedly gave him the opportunity to learn theatrical know-how, as well as develop a strong dramatic interest. His work has been compared with that of Menotti, and indeed there is some similarity between his one-act opera *Varjo* (*Shadow*), a naturalistic thriller and Menotti's *The Consul*. There is a strong Italian flavour to Pylkkänen's music. It is extremely well written for the human voice, which is given every opportunity to demonstrate its melodic and romantic capabilities. However, this type of music is not expected from the pen of a contemporary composer, and I doubt whether Pylkkänen's operas, in spite of their rich orchestration and fine vocal writing, will become established outside Scandinavia. Part of the reason for this assumption is based on the fact that the plots have a strongly national character which will not be easy to recreate, even if a first-class translation can be provided.

In his present capacity as artistic director of the Finnish National Opera, there is every possibility that Pylkkänen's future works will offer more to contemporary audiences. He is certainly one of Finland's major musical figures.

XII

FINNISH MUSIC is not without its tragedies, the most poignant of which was probably the death at the age of sixteen of HEIKKI SUOLAHTI (1920–36). This prodigy had already begun composing potentially significant music. His *Symphonia Piccola* has been played in the United States although the composer died before having the opportunity of hearing any of his music publicly performed. Sibelius said of him: 'Finland lost with Heikki Suolahti one of her greatest musical talents'.

We can be grateful that Suolahti's musical gift began to flower at such an early age, for had a similar fate overtaken JOONAS KOKKONEN (b 1921), Finland would have suffered the loss of one of her finest creative artists.

At the time of writing this book—the middle 1960's—Kokkonen and Bergman occupy the twin positions as the creative giants in Finnish musical culture. Their personalities have certain surface facets in common. Both are widely read, intellectual and reticent in public. Their approach to music, however, is fundamentally different. Whereas Bergman applies logic, Kokkonen is a mystic. Whereas Bergman has turned his back on accepted musical forms, and experimented with new sounds, Kokkonen's music has its roots in the classical symphonic style, some of his work appearing to critics as a natural continuation of the sym-

Olavi Pesonen

Erkki Salmenhaara

Kari Rydman

Matti Rautio

Bengt Johansson

Kaj Chydenius

Seppo Nummi

Einar Englund

Nils-Erik Fougstedt

Pentti Melanen

Aulikki Rautavaara

Pianists Rhondda Gillespie and Yonty Solomon, with Ragnar Meinander (centre) of the Finnish Ministry of Education, during the 1967 Camden Festival in London

Tom Krause

Leif Segerstam in action

Taru Valjakka

Kim Borg

phonic ideals of Sibelius. Whereas Bergman has become increasingly drawn towards the potential of the human voice, Kokkonen has produced his finest work in the symphonic field, displaying a tremendous talent for string writing.

In 1957 his *Music for Strings* was heard for the first time, and immediately recognized as a work of genius. In many ways this work belies its title. In reality it is a symphony both in structure and conception. Perhaps, in common with Brahms, Kokkonen stood in awe of the word 'symphony', not wishing to produce a work in this genre until he had achieved absolute maturity. He himself described his *Music for Strings* as belonging to his chamber-music period, which includes the Piano Trio of 1948 and a masterly Piano Quintet, first heard in 1953. Even a passing acquaintance with his First String Quartet, completed in 1959, is sufficient to amply demonstrate his symphonic approach to chamber form; the Second Quartet, composed in 1966, is one of the finest contemporary examples of concentrated string writing. Nevertheless, it is the music that matters and this is music by a man who has something important and cogent to say. His string writing is expressive and serene, yet with an underlying apprehension which reflects the uneasiness which pervades our contemporary life.

Kokkonen was elected to the Academy of Finland upon the death of Uuno Klami and became chairman of the Society of Finnish Composers in 1965. In 1959 he had been appointed Professor of Composition at the Sibelius Academy, one of the most distinguished posts in Finnish musical circles. The following year saw the completion of his First Symphony. Two years later he was commissioned by the Festival Strings of Lucerne to compose a work for their 1962 festival. This string symphony, in fact his Third Symphony, entitled *Sinfonia da camera*, has attracted world wide attention, and through it Kokkonen's name has become widely known outside Scandinavia. The *Sinfonia da camera* is based on the B-A-C-H progression and makes free use of a linear technique. Kokkonen has described Bach as his

4

greatest teacher and this work is, perhaps, a tribute to Bach from his distinguished admirer.

It is significant that Kokkonen's approach to instrumentation has deliberately avoided the over-use of percussion. Instead, he is continually exploring the many permutations and combinations possible for conventional instruments, especially strings. More recently, he has taken an interest in vocal writing, and should this develop it may well be a fascinating experience to compare the results with the works of Bergman.

In the meantime, it is sufficient to describe Joonas Kokkonen as a comparable Scandinavian composer to Benjamin Britten in England, with a special emphasis on string writing and musical roots.

The Second String Quartet is now available in Philips Modern Music Series, played by London's Delmé String Quartet, who gave the English premiere in November, 1967.

XIII

ONLY TWENTY-FIVE miles or so from Helsinki is the town of Järvenpää, where MAURI HONGISTO (b 1921) is the principal conductor for the local choir as well as being a piano teacher. Hongisto was born in Tampere where he attended the secondary school and business college. The war years interrupted his career, but demonstrated his qualities of leadership since he was promoted to the rank of Platoon Commander in the Karelia Isthmus during the Continuation War 1942–44.

After the war he joined the conducting class at the Sibelius Academy in 1951, also studying composition, for which he was awarded a diploma in 1958.

Hongisto's output includes an early violin concerto, composed in 1954, a piano concerto composed the following year and several large-scale works, including cantatas for choirs both with and without orchestra. In view of his work as a piano teacher, it is not surprising that Hongisto has also composed a great many piano pieces for children.

Few composers have devoted as much attention to the intelligent introduction of musical appreciation in schools as MATTI RAUTIO (b 1922). It is not surprising that his music shows a special influence of Carl Orff, himself a great reformer of school music. Rautio's little ballet *Sininen haikara* (*The Blue Stork*) is probably his most popular work in Finland, and it is noteworthy that he has made elegant use of Orff's instrumentation techniques in this Chinese fairy-tale. Rautio has also composed a large quantity of piano music, much of which belongs to the kind of music which the gifted amateur enjoys playing at home. He makes use of folk rhythms and syncopations in his Divertimento for cello and orchestra, where the third movement—a delicious can-can—is full of fun, with its juxtaposing of upper-register cello solo and tuba. This little four movement work is a witty, crafts-manlike and effective addition to the repertoire.

At the moment of writing this book, I learned that Matti Rautio is working on the score of a piano concerto which at this stage in his musical development may well be a significant work.

In 1959, another Finnish composer, OSMO LINDEMAN (b 1929) was awarded a UNESCO Sibelius Scholarship to the Munich Music Academy, where he studied composition with Carl Orff. He had already won a diploma in composition at the Sibelius Academy in his native city of Helsinki, where he was also highly thought of as a pianist. However, it was his First Symphony, *Sinfonia inornata*, which especially attracted attention after its first performance by the Helsinki City Symphony Orchestra in 1959. This Symphony and the String Trio composed the previous year shows a concentrated and economical use of thematic material and a thoughtful serious approach to thematic development.

Lindeman remained at Munich until 1960, and his next two works are in the nature of experiments in writing for percussion and brass. Each is dated 1962, the first being a Partita for Percussion which was followed by *Counterpoint for Brass*.

Lindeman is not a prolific composer and has been mainly successful in his incidental music for films and theatre. In fact, two of his film scores were awarded 'Jussi', the Finnish equivalent of an Oscar.

More recently both the Second Piano Concerto (1965) and his String Quartet (1966) show a tendency to experiment with sound, which I find to be at the expense of the musical core of the works.

44

For example, the string writing in both works demands considerably greater technical perfection and greater exactitude in timing than would be possible in most performances. In the Piano Concerto there are pages in which there is so much division not only in the strings but throughout the orchestra that a great deal must inevitably be lost, or become confusing to the listener. I have the feeling that Lindeman is looking for his own individual style and that his best work is yet to come.

XIV

ON THE occasion of my first visit to Finland, for the 1964 Sibelius Festival, I attended a programme of contemporary Finnish music presented by Finnish Radio in Helsinki's impressive Hall of Knights. It was this concert which triggered off my intense interest in and appreciation of Finnish music.

Kokkonen's *Sinfonia da camera* I already knew, but music by the younger generation was entirely new to me. One of the most beautiful and stimulating works was the Oboe Quartet by EINOJUHANI RAUTAVAARA (b 1928), who has already established himself in the forefront of the younger Scandinavian composers.

Rautavaara studied composition at the Sibelius Academy with Aarre Merikanto, after which his talent enabled him to obtain grants from the Koussevitzky Foundation and the Finlandia Foundation to spend some years studying in the United States.

The first work which brought him public acclaim was his *Requiem in our Time*, for wind instruments and percussion, which won an American competition for wind ensembles in 1954. His music was soon being heard at the annual ISCM festivals, where it soon became apparent that he had a special emotional understanding for string writing.

Rautavaara is a member of one of the most important musical

families in Finland, which included Pentti Rautavaara (1911–65), one of the foremost cellists in Scandinavia and the internationally famous soprano, Aulikki Rautavaara. His home life is that of a busy musical family, for his wife Mariaheidi has also gained international fame as a Wagnerian soprano and an interpreter of Kilpinen's songs.

Rautavaara has successfully composed music on large and small canvases. A fine pianist, he has written several small works for the instrument, one of the most satisfying and attractive being his *Icons Suite* composed in 1955, when the composer was in the United States. The six short movements are miniature tone poems, each depicting a separate icon visualized in terms of music by the homesick young composer.

Although the titles—*eg The Death of the Mother of God, The Holy Women at the Sepulchre* and *The Archangel Michael fighting the Anti-Christ*—are perhaps a little forbidding, the music is straightforward, extremely pianistic and immediately interesting. The lugubrious, dark purple quality of the chords and deep sforzando trills, which diminish into an impressive silence in *The Black Madonna of Blakernaya*, superbly picture this ancient church in Constantinople, blackened by candle smoke and scarred by centuries of human history. On the other hand, *Two Village Saints*, taken from the door of an old icon cabinet in a simple village church, is jocular and light-hearted, easily bringing to the imagination the simplicity of the country background and the fun of Easter weddings in the countryside.

In a thoroughly unpretentious way, this little suite is an excellent introduction not only to the composer but to the contemporary idiom he uses so skilfully. *Icons*, as indeed Englund's Introduction and Toccata, have been successfully included by Rhondda Gillespie in recitals both in England and Germany.

At the other end of the musical scale, as well as demonstrating Rautavaara's wide cultural abilities, is his opera *Kaivos* (*The Mine*), for which he also provided an impressive libretto. This is the most important operatic work by a Finnish composer to date, although it is still waiting for a staged public performance.

Kaivos was presented on Finnish Television in 1963, two years after its completion, and has since been shown several times on the small screen. Although the production and standard of singing are very good, much of the dramatic impact of the work is lost by the impersonality of cinematic techniques. I am sure that, given a good translation, *Kaivos* would be a highly successful opera on any international stage.

The plot concerns a mining community, many miles from the capital of an unspecified (presumably Iron Curtain) country. There has been a revolt against the State, during which the revolutionary leaders have temporarily gained control and asked for active support from the country as a whole. The miners are in sympathy with the revolutionaries, and turn against their Prefect, or Party foreman, who is depicted as a thoroughly human, if idealistic man, taking as their leader an outlawed guerilla who joins them against his better judgment, because he feels that they need him.

He brings with him into the mine his mistress, Maria, who is immediately despised and ostracized by the other women of the community. In her despair, Maria releases the Prefect from his bonds, and—when the community, including her lover, take refuge inside the mine—she purposely abstains from informing them of a news broadcast she has heard (while they were all out looking for the Prefect) to the effect that the State had quelled the revolution and had promised free pardons to all citizens on condition that they would give up their leaders.

The outcome of the opera is inevitably one of tragedy, but the drama is taken to its highest possible intensity during the claustrophobic final scene deep inside the mine. The music has a searing, passionate quality lightened by the love scene between the two main characters and some comic moments by a couple of the miners. The opera is strong meat, and in the tradition of contemporary dramatic works for the theatre.

Rautavaara's greatest quality is his obvious love of cultivated beauty. His Third Symphony is a surprising dual homage to Bruckner and Berg, in which the romanticism of the former is allied to the modernistic style of writing of the latter, yet retaining the composer's individual personality. Berg's dramatic sense has undoubtedly been an important influence in Rautavaara's work which has also benefited from his work as a music critic.

A noteworthy fact about Rautavaara's compositions is that musicians immediately wish to perform them. A recent example of this is that his Third String Quartet was unanimously chosen to win the chamber-music section of a competition for new Finnish compositions, organized by the London Borough of Camden and that the members of the Delmé String Quartet felt an immediate rapport with this one-movement work. As well as introducing it in London and Helsinki, the Delmé Quartet have recorded it in Philips Modern Music Series and it has been published in London by Josef Weinberger Ltd. It is dedicated to the Delmé String Quartet.

Rautavaara is still under forty years of age, and at the height of his creative powers. It will be interesting to assess him again in another twenty years.

XV

WHEN RAUTAVAARA'S *Requiem in our Time* was given first prize in the 1954 Thor Johnsson Contest in Cincinnati, the second prize was presented to USKO MERILÄINEN (b 1930) for his Partita for brass. In fact winning prizes in competitions has been a feature of the musical achievements of this highly individual composer.

He was born on January 27 in Tampere, sharing his birth date with Mozart, and originally studied in the Music School there from 1946–1950, after which he continued his studies at the Sibelius Academy in Helsinki where he qualified as a composer and also as a conductor under the joint tutelage of Aarre Merikanto and Leo Funtek. He then went to Switzerland to study under Vladimir Vogel under whose guidance he soon became familiar with twelve-tone serialism.

Meriläinen is an extremely intelligent and complex personality, and this is reflected in his music. He is an introvert, continually seeking after truth with uncompromising inner strength.

It is this continual struggle, not only to find the right means of expression but to ensure the validity of what is expressed, that gives Meriläinen's work its intellectual appeal. Yet underlying this struggle there is a warm love of humanity and a bubbling sense of humour which all too rarely comes to the surface. His large-scale works require great concentration on the part of the listener, which is amply repaid.

One exception is the Piano Concerto, written in 1955 as a wedding present for an amateur Finnish pianist, Olli Tenkanen, who gave the first performance, after the work had been declared unplayable by several professionals. The opening theme achieves a jaunty sense of apparent syncopation by means of a strong accent on the first beat of each 5/4 bar.

The solo writing is rhythmic and technically brilliant whilst the orchestra is primarily occupied with the task of emphasising rather than clarifying the soloist's impetuosity. The second movement is impressionistic, vaguely reminiscent of Debussy, with the soloist again as the main protagonist. A rollicking finale completes this very attractive concerto which was first heard outside Finland at the opening concert of the Camden (St Pancras) Arts Festival in February 1967 when Rhondda Gillespie was soloist and London's Royal Philharmonic Orchestra was conducted by Walter Süsskind.

At the same festival, Meriläinen's Second Piano Sonata received its world premiere, played by Yonty Solomon, in the presence of the composer, this work having been awarded first prize in the piano section of the festival competition, already referred to in the last chapter. It is dedicated to Yonty Solomon, and has been published in London by Josef Weinberger Ltd.

Meriläinen lives in his native Tampere in a beautiful house surrounded by trees and overlooking a lake. In winter, he and his family cannot leave the house except on skis, and his close proximity to Nature has played an important role in adding breadth and a rugged individualism to his work.

Besides the English performances of his works, there has been great interest expressed in Germany where his *Epyllion* was commissioned by the publishers Bote & Bock, and was performed in Berlin with notable success. His Second Symphony has also been accepted for publication by the same firm. A Chamber Concerto for violin, two string orchestras and percussion won third prize in the AIDEM competition at Florence in 1962, but even more important was the Wihuri-Sibelius Composition Contest prize awarded for his ballet *Arius*, an essentially symbolic work depicting Man against the background of his modern existence.

As a practical musician, Meriläinen has conducted the orchestras of Kuopio and Tampere, as well as training the choir in the Finnish National Opera and conducting musical performances at the Tampere Workers' Theatre, where he undoubtedly gained experience in the composition of music for theatrical productions and films. One of his film scores was awarded a Finnish Oscar.

Philips Modern Music Series have now issued two discs devoted to contemporary Finnish music, with the accent on the works heard in London at the 1967 Camden Festival. Meriläinen is represented on each disc—the Piano Concerto on the orchestral, and the Second Piano Sonata on the chamber record—the artists being Rhondda Gillespie with the Royal Philharmonic Orchestra conducted by Walter Süsskind in the Concerto, and Yonty Solomon in the Sonata.

Meriläinen has achieved a great deal for a man in his middle thirties. He is still seeking a true understanding of himself and his place in the world of music. When he finds this, he should produce works of lasting value.

XVI

IT IS difficult to fully evaluate the importance of SEPPO NUMMI (b 1932) in the musical life of Finland. He is one of those quicksilver, elusive, yet ever-present-when-needed characters, who leave the imprint of their personality and prolific ideas wherever they go. As a music critic, Nummi has a reputation for sharp observation and catholic taste. He may tend to side more with the tonal and warm-blooded composers than with their cerebral colleagues but he is always objective. Throughout his writing—which, of course, I have only read in translation—there is a strong love of music and appreciation of the difficulties which professional musicians have to face.

Apart from his reviews, musical essays and editorship of books on musical matters, Seppo Nummi finds time and energy to lecture extensively, travel to the major foreign festivals and also organize the annual music festivals and seminars in Jyväskylä, the principal town of central Finland. The importance of this festival can best be assessed by the large number of visitors from all parts of the world who flock there every summer. Japanese kimonos, African robes and every conceivable variation in Western dress become as commonplace as the babble of different tongues in the bars and restaurants and entrance hall to the beautiful university campus where the festival events take place.

In 1966 Jyväskylä was chosen by UNESCO as the ideal location for the final seminar of their far reaching East-West Major Project. Recitals, operas and orchestral concerts were filled to capacity and, despite the fact that up to then there was no well organized office staff to deal with the many large and small problems which inevitably arise on these occasions, every problem was sorted out smoothly, very often by the charm and personal efficiency of Seppo Nummi. If the Jyväskylä Festival achieves the international recognition it so richly deserves, it will owe a large proportion of praise for this achievement to him.

In the realm of composition, Nummi has concentrated on songs, many of which have their roots in folk traditions and all of which show a rare appreciation for the melodic qualities of the human voice. He has composed over 230 songs, as well as twenty madrigals and music for radio.

A composer whose creative output may well reach fruition in future years is ILKKA TANELI KUUSISTO (b 1933) who has devoted himself principally to choral and church music. In one respect he could be said to be following in his father's footsteps for the young Kuusisto is the organist for the Meilahti congregation in Helsinki, where his father Taneli Kuusisto holds the post of organist at the Töölö Church. Ilkka studied at the Sibelius Academy under Aarre Merikanto and Nils-Eric Fougstedt and was awarded an organist diploma in 1954 and a teaching degree in 1958, after which he went to New York for a year to study at the Union Theological Seminary's School of Sacred Music, under Seth Bingham. The following year was spent studying in Germany.

His compositions include three preludes for brass, choir and organ, various songs both for solo voice and ensemble, several organ compositions and a Duo for flute and cello.

As well as being conductor of the South Finland Student Corporation's Mixed Chorus, the Academic Singers and the Helsinki Police Singers, Ilkka Kuusisto is also chorusmaster of the Finnish National Opera in Helsinki.

Ilkka Kuusisto is by no means a square: he is very much a part of the little band of progressive composers who are now making their impact on the more acute musical sensitivity of Helsinki's old guard.

In 1964 he shared a concert of new music with REIJO EINARI JYRKIÄINEN (b 1934), a Finnish composer who has primarily experimented with electronic music and *musique concrète*.

Jyrkiäinen was born in a part of Karelia which is now within the territory of the USSR. He went to school in Imatra, joining the Sibelius Academy in the autumn of 1956 where he studied piano with Margaretha Tandefelt, orchestration with Nils-Eric Fougstedt and composition under Joonas Kokkonen. He won a composition diploma in 1963 just before attending his second Summer School for New Music at Darmstadt. Also in 1963 he visited Bilthoven's electronic music studio for special study with Gottfried Mikael König. The following year as well as at Darmstadt he studied with Henri Tousseur in the Munich electronic music studio.

I think it is significant that apart from his practical musical studies, Jyrkiäinen was for five years at the university of Helsinki where he studied theoretical philosophy, aesthetics and music under Professor Erik Tawaststjerna, a man of great intellect and musicality. Jyrkiäinen's analysis of Schoenberg's twelve-tone serialism in the Variations for Orchestra, Op 31, won him the candidate's degree in the Humanities in 1963.

It is not surprising that his present occupation is as 'tone-master' at the Finnish Broadcasting Corporation where his special knowledge of tape recordings is frequently called for, as well as his special capabilities as producer of *musica nova* concerts.

Up to date, he has composed only six works, the first and longest being a String Sextet which dates from 1962—just before his first visit to Darmstadt. The following year—with the Darmstadt influence newly upon him—saw *Sounds I* and *Sounds II*, both in the medium of *musique concrète*, and also *Idiopostic*, a nine-minute work of electronic music which I find very effective as atmospheric sound, evoking a mixture of cosmic and Hitchcock impressions.

The years 1964 and 1965 each saw the production of one work. The first, *For Four*, is scored for clarinet, guitar, violin and percussion, whilst *Contradictions* is an eight-minute piece for flute, clarinet, guitar, percussion and string quartet. This is a far more interesting work, both in instrumental colouring and logical thought, than its predecessor, and it would appear that Jyrkiäinen has followed in the footsteps of many young composers and shaken the tape recorder out of his system, having first utilised it as a means of physically mixing sound colours.

An extremely likeable and alert conversationalist, he lives with his wife and four children in Tapiola just outside Helsinki.

Arto Noras, the young Finnish
cellist, second prizewinner of the
1966 Tschaikowsky Competition
in Moscow, and hailed by London
critics as one of the great cellists of
our time, after his British debut in
November, 1967.

Matti Lehtinen

Martti Talvela

Anita Välkki

Jorma Panula

Kai Maasalo, Head of Music for the
Finnish Radio

Harald Andersen

The Finnish Radio Chamber Choir

Paavo Berglund

Kim Borg as Count Almaviva

Tauno Hannikainen

Paavo Berglund and his wife, Kirsti

Conductor Walter Süsskind, who conducts the Royal Philharmonic Orchestra in Heininen's Adagio, and accompanies Heather Harper on the piano in Segerstam's Song Cycle 'Three Leaves of Grass,' on Philips Modern Music record series. He had performed both works at their world premieres in London.

The South African pianist Yonty Solomon who gave the world premiere of Meriläinen's Piano Sonata No. 2 in London, and has also recorded the work for Philips Modern Music Series.

Composer Paavo Heininen (right) and conductor Walter Süsskind acknowledge the applause after Heininen's Adagio had received its world premiere, at the opening concert of the 1967 Camden Festival in London, by the Royal Philharmonic Orchestra.

XVII

DURING THE centenary celebrations of the birth of Sibelius, which culminated in the 1965 Sibelius Violin Competition in Helsinki, Finnish composers were invited to submit a work which could be used as a set piece for the contestants. It, of course, had to be a composition which would test the young competitors' musicianship and, at the same time, tax their technique. The work chosen was the *Cadenza* for unaccompanied violin by AULIS SALLINEN (b 1935) who is the intendant of the Finnish Radio Symphony Orchestra.

Sallinen studied composition at the Sibelius Academy under Aarre Merikanto and Joonas Kokkonen. Some of his earlier works made extensive use of the twelve-tone system, but he seems to have abandoned this form of discipline and allowed his musical imagination freer rein.

Sallinen's delicacy when dealing with the orchestra is well demonstrated in his *14 Juventas Variations*, composed in 1963. This work is a model of economy, in which I feel that every bar was revised and refined to the point where all inessentials have been eliminated. The first four variations build up to an emotional climax which resolves into the fugal section of Variation 5. There also is some beautifully sustained string writing in Variation 9, and my main criticism of the work is that the variations are sometimes too short: I personally would like to savour them at greater length than just become briefly aware of them.

Sallinen has a natural feeling for string writing which is also to be found in his two quartets, his *Elegy to Sebastian Knight* and Variations for cello and orchestra and his *Metamorphosis* for piano and chamber orchestra, where the string writing is particularly interesting.

Since 1960 Sallinen has been secretary of the Society of Composers of Finland and sits on their board. In this connection his important position with the Finnish Radio, together with his genial personality must make him an extremely useful liaison between the two bodies.

At first glance, KARI RYDMAN'S (b 1936) position in Finland's contemporary music scene would appear to be fairly straightforward. Although he is a man of apparent contradictions, upon closer examination these prove to dovetail one with another as interrelated facets of an extremely complex personality.

Rydman studied at Helsinki University, and much of his time at present is occupied as teacher of music to an industrial arts school and a secondary school in Helsinki. He has edited several books on musical matters and history, and also made a reputation for himself as a sharp-tongued critic for a daily newspaper in Helsinki. His compositions range from strikingly original chamber music to very successful pop records which are noteworthy for their unaffected simplicity and naïvety.

Rydman has often described himself as a self-taught composer, his first work, *Sonata I*, being his own way 'to unite impressions from Darmstadt to cantilena melodies' to use his own words. His most ambitious work is the *Great Quartet* which in fact comprises his String Quartets Nos 2, 3 and 4. I must admit that, although I found this work interesting from the point of view of string sound, I could find no parallel between the Quartet No 2 (the first part of the *Great Quartet*) and Beethoven's C sharp minor Quartet, which, the composer tells us, was its spiritual model. The work is dedicated to Kaj Chydenius, (q.v.).

For my own part I found Rydman's *Sonata IV* for violin, guitar, clarinet and percussion more stimulating. His strikingly original clarinet writing, which is reminiscent but by no means imitative of the Witches' Sabbath from Berlioz's *Symphonie fantastique*, is of a very high level. The second movement is memorable for evocative percussion and pizzicato guitar scoring, and indeed the work as a whole has a quality of controlled freedom and improvisation with a loose yet sensitive rein.

Kari Rydman is seeking his own medium of expression, and it is difficult to prophesy where this medium is leading him. Of one thing I am certain, we shall be hearing much more from him during the next decade.

There is no question as to the direction in which PAAVO JOHANNES HEININEN (b 1938) is moving in his compositions. His confidence in scoring for a huge orchestra, together with his intellectual maturity as a musician, indicate that his music—at least in his own mind—is to be composed against a large canvas with every possible permutation and combination of sound-colours from his palette. Heininen studied at Helsinki University and at the Sibelius Academy, gaining his composition diploma in 1960, but he has greatly enlarged his musical horizons by studying at the Hochschule in Cologne and at the Juilliard School of Music in New York. A first-class pianist who worked at the Finnish Opera from 1959–60, he undoubtedly gave himself a thorough grounding in operatic and vocal techniques. It is interesting to see from his list of compositions that only two works—*Canto di natale* for soprano and piano (1961) and *Easter Passacaglia* composed in 1963 for baritone solo, mixed chorus and organ, specially for a television play—make use of the human voice. This composer does not waste musical impressions, and his years at the Opera in Helsinki have yet to bear fruit, perhaps in a grandiose opera.

Heininen's music has the uncompromising attitude one would expect from a musician who has studied with such professors as Petzold, Zimmermann, Steuermann and Persichetti. Even his relatively early Quintet for flute, saxophone, piano, vibraphone and percussion, composed in 1961, shows a tendency in the percussion writing to burst away from the field of chamber music. Nevertheless, its vitality and colour and the manner in which he uses the piano to hold the looser elements together, as well as his highly developed sense of timing and rhythm help to off-set the large amount of flutter-tonguing for the saxophone and weighty percussion writing.

It is in the orchestral field that Heininen has made his greatest impact, and in Finland he has been described as a virtuoso composer. His *Adagio: concerto for orchestra in the form of Variations*, composed in 1963, was described as a homage to Mahler when first performed in Helsinki the following year. The revised version was awarded the joint orchestral prize in the competition already referred to, and was first heard outside Scandinavia at the opening concert of the Camden (St Pancras) Arts Festival in 1967 by the Royal Philharmonic Orchestra conducted by Walter Süsskind. The same players have recorded the work for Philips Modern Music Series. It is dedicated jointly to Walter Süsskind and Denby Richards.

At present Paavo Heininen is on the staff of the Sibelius Academy having previously been piano professor at the Turku Institute of Music.

XVIII

I HAVE a theory that the apparently wildest and most uninhibited of artists are basically the most conventional people. There is something in their make-up which rebels against society and erupts in the form of avantgarde productions, but once the artist has got this out of his system he settles down and begins to write or paint works which are both intelligible and straightforward. This is only a theory and might even be described as wishful thinking, but to some extent it sums up my impressions of Finland's *enfant terrible*, HENRIK OTTO DONNER (b 1939). The Establishment finds it very difficult to take him seriously in spite of the fact that he studied composition at the Sibelius Academy under Fougstedt and Kokkonen. Needless to say, he also spent some time at Bilthoven under König for electronic music and also went to the Siemens Studio and studied later with György Liget.

Donner is a first-class trumpet player and has worked as a free-lance jazz musician in Helsinki. He has also produced 'happenings' which have shocked, excited and become seven-day wonders, whilst at the same time inevitably diverting interest from the more serious side of his nature. Nevertheless, Donner is talked of with great affection and admiration by his contemporaries.

His *Cantata Profana* (1962) for soprano, tenor, baritone and chamber ensemble is an example of cocking a snoot at established musical ideology, as also is his Symphony No 1, subtitled *Hommage à Ives*, composed in 1964 for string orchestra, guitar, harp and electronic organ. This latter work, with its irreverent quotes from Mozart's *Eine kleine Nachtmusik* juxtaposed with ungainly intervals and glissandos, seems to go out of its way to offend, yet beneath its rebellious surface there is the mind and emotions of a genuine musician of stimulating originality.

Donner is always experimenting but not merely for the sake of experimentation: to him it is a means of clarifying his musical language. He believes very strongly in providing opportunities for improvisation which enable musicians to add their own personalities within the framework of his inspiration; he is interested in the stereophonic effects to be achieved both from the placing of his musicians and from having them move whilst performing, as in his *Idiogramme* (1963) composed for tape, twenty musicians and promenade room! When he has clarified his musical stimuli I think that we may well expect to hear a great deal more of this young composer.

Another composer who is similarly searching for his own means of expression, and who has also been drawn towards jazz and popular music, is KAJ CHYDENIUS (b 1939), the son of a Finnish economist who told his musical offspring 'musicians cannot make enough money'. Accordingly, young Chydenius studied languages at the Economist High School as well as taking music at the Sibelius Academy and Helsinki University under the indefatigable Erik Tawaststjerna. He began writing musical criticism in 1959, and soon came to the conclusion that young men of his own age were writing worthwhile music and not being appreciated either by their elders or other critics. For this reason, in 1962, he offered himself to the *Hufudstadsbladet*, the leading Swedish-language daily in Helsinki, and became their music critic.

Shortly after this, partly through his influence as a journalist, he was able to arrange for collaboration between several of the younger generation of Finnish composers including Kari Rydman, Henrik Otto Donner and Erkki Salmenhaara (q.v.) These young musicians met regularly to study and listen to the contemporary musical trends from outside Finland.

In 1964 Chydenius became president of the Finnish section of the International Society of Contemporary Music, and under his guidance a collaboration between all the Scandinavian ISCMs became an established fact.

He soon elaborated on this theme of collaboration for young artists, and started the Finnish Students' Centre in Helsinki with the intention of bringing young Finnish musicians together with their contemporaries in the theatre, film and art worlds, for he felt that the musicians were still too much cut off from current trends in artistic ideology. In this way he hoped to bring all young artists together in such a way that they could receive stimuli from all possible sources.

In 1964 Chydenius first heard a record of the Beatles and was impressed by their impact on the public. He began to lose faith in the approach of serious musicians to express the mood and purpose of the world in which we live, and came to the conclusion that both serious music and the pop music of the Beatles had a similar but not lasting effect on different cultural levels. He began to look inside himself for a new way of bringing important cultural ideas to a large public and decided that songs, especially within a theatrical framework were the answer. Since then he has composed over seventy songs, many of which have been made for use by the Finnish Student Theatre in Helsinki.

In 1965 he married Kaisa Korhonen the artistic director of the Student Theatre, and later he was appointed administrative director there. In 1966 Helsinki had its first taste of this collaboration when *Lapualaisooppera* was produced at the Student Theatre to packed and enthusiastic audiences. Although Chydenius' music to this bitingly satirical comment on the politically torn Finland of the 1930's is not especially striking, it nevertheless is absolutely right within the context of the play. His wife proved to be an excellent interpreter of his musical idiom, and there is no doubt that as a team they will be extremely successful in future ventures.

It would seem that as a composer Chydenius has settled himself firmly on the side of pop art and the theatre. With his background and wide knowledge he should be an invaluable champion of contemporary trends in his chosen medium.

XIX

A NAME which has continually cropped up in this book either as a writer or teacher is Erik Verner Tawaststjerna, whose importance and influence cannot be over-estimated. He was born in 1916 in the little town of Mikkeli on Lake Saimaa, one of the most extensive of Europe's lake systems. He matriculated in 1934, received his MA in 1958 and his PhD in 1960. His first study was as a pianist at the Sibelius Academy in 1934–37, but since then he has travelled extensively all over the world both to study and lecture.

His erudition, which first showed itself in his music criticisms in the *Helsingin Sanomat* and later in his books on Sibelius and other composers, is unquestioned. At present he is professor of music at Helsinki University, as well as deputy chairman of the Music Society. Tawaststjerna has the practical knowledge of music so often lacking in musicologists. As a concert pianist he first performed in Helsinki in 1943, since when he has given concerts in the Soviet Union, Austria, Norway, Paris, Brussels and Copenhagen. However, for the past decade he has occupied himself mainly with encouraging and teaching young musicians in Finland, and also with his monumental treatises on the life and works of Jean Sibelius.

Perhaps his most gifted pupil, and certainly his most devout disciple, is ERKKI SALMENHAARA (b 1941) who is at present his assistant in the Faculty of Music of Helsinki University. Salmen-haara is also widely read as a critic, but his most important contribution is as one of Finland's most fascinating composers.

He studied composition at the Sibelius Academy under Joonas Kokkonen and then privately with György Ligeti in Austria. His doctor's degree was granted on his thesis on György Ligeti's works.

Salmenhaara's compositions show an uncanny understanding for string textures. His *Elegia II* for two string quartets is one of the most beautiful and thoughtful works I have ever heard for strings. There is an introspection in his music, a determination to find the perfect manner of expression which is both endearing and mystical. His humour lurks deep but sure beneath the surface, rarely being permitted to enter the more serious vein of his musical thought.

In common with many contemporary composers, Salmenhaara tends to write the almost impossible. He divides his strings in the Second Symphony and elsewhere into fastidiously small numbers, giving each player fantastically difficult passages, any one of which when played inaccurately could serve to blur and distort the whole. With an orchestra of virtuosi, a conductor of genius and perfect conditions of performance, after many rehearsals, the result could be astonishingly stimulating. However, there can be no compromise, and anything short of perfection leads to be-wildering chaos.

My own opinion is that Salmenhaara is the most sensitive and potentially important of Finland's younger composers. His music does what only great music can do, it takes one by the spine and sets up a tingling which eventually possesses one entirely with the full agreement and co-operation of the mental faculties.

It would be presumptuous and impossible to predict a future musical direction for a man within whom burns the spark of genius, but I have the feeling that Salmenhaara will take symphonic form along new paths and to new heights, and I urge everybody who reads this book to look out for his name on concert pro-grammes.

XX

IF PRODIGALITY and achievement can be taken as indications of success, then LEIF SEGERSTAM (b 1944) seems set on a road which leads towards great things. This quiet, unassuming young all-round musician has an inner determination to leave his mark on the musical world, which I am confident he will achieve.

Segerstam was born in Vaasa, one of Finland's larger cities, and became a student at the Sibelius Academy at the age of eight in the preparatory division, remaining at the Academy until 1963. During that time he studied violin and piano as well as conducting and composition, his teachers for the latter subject being Nils-Erik Fougstedt, Einar Englund and Joonas Kokkonen. In 1963 Segerstam graduated with diplomas in conducting and violin, and was granted a special scholarship to the Juilliard School of Music in New York, where he obtained a conducting diploma in 1964 and a post-graduate diploma in 1965. His Juilliard courses in conducting were under Jean Morel and there is no doubt that he also gained a great deal of knowledge and experience at the 1964 summer course in Aspen, Colorado, under Walter Süsskind. In 1962, he had also taken part in a summer course in Finland in recorder playing.

His musicianship resulted in scholarships from many sources, including the Swedish Cultural Foundation in 1963 and 1964 and the Asla-Fulbright Scholarship for the same period, which were supplemented by a Finnish State grant in 1964 and a Finlandia Foundation Scholarship in 1964–5. Also in this period he won a scholarship from the Juilliard School, where he also gained a teaching fellowship in the department of Literature and Materials of Music. In 1964 Segerstam was also awarded a Finnish Composers' Society grant.

In 1960, when he was sixteen, Segerstam won first prize in the Young Nordic Talent Competition as a violinist, and two years later won first prize in the Maj-Lind Competition for Finnish pianists under thirty years of age. In 1964 he was a semi-finalist in the Mitropoulos Competition.

His début as a violinist in 1962 in Helsinki was followed by a tour of Finland. This was repeated in 1964 before he left for New York where he gave a recital in the Liederkranz Hall. The following year, again as a violinist, Segerstam gave recitals in the Judson Hall in New York and in Aspen. As a concerto soloist he has played in Helsinki and Tampere as well as on Finnish radio and television. In the spring season of 1963 he conducted fifteen performances of Rossini's *The Barber of Seville* in Tampere as well as concerts at the Sibelius Academy and at the Aspen Music Festival and Juilliard School of Music with the Student Symphony Orchestras. In 1964 and 1965 he conducted concerts with the Juilliard Orchestra Players at the International House Auditorium in New York, after the second of which he returned to Finland, where he conducted the Radio Symphony Orchestra, shortly afterwards being appointed regular conductor at the Finnish National Opera.

Throughout this active existence as a performing musician both as a student and later a professional, Leif Segerstam has also found time for composition. His first work was a *Legend* for string orchestra, written in memory of Nils-Erik Fougstedt in 1960. Up to date his work has been mainly concerned with chamber music and songs, several of which have been heard on the Finnish radio with the composer accompanying his sister at the piano.

My first acquaintance with this talented young man came as a result of my asking Anita Välkki in Helsinki for her opinion regarding young Finnish composers. She enthusiastically praised some of Segerstam's songs and introduced me to him. Shortly after this when I expressed an interest in hearing his Second String Quartet three members of the City Symphony Orchestra immediately volunteered to join the composer in giving me a private performance. This work with its warm, well integrated string writing also attracted the attention of the Delmé String Quartet when I showed it to them in London.

More recently, Segerstam's music has moved away from the tonal, and the piano writing in his three soprano settings of texts from Walt Whitman's *Leaves of Grass* which won the song cycle section of the Camden (St Pancras) Festival competition, is uncompromising and vital. These songs received their first performance at the 1967 Festival when they were sung by the English soprano Heather Harper accompanied by Walter Süsskind, who in this way demonstrated his personal faith in his former conducting pupil. This cycle, which is dedicated to Heather Harper, is available on the Philips Modern Music Series Finnish discs, performed by Heather Harper with Walter Süsskind at the piano, and published by Josef Weinberger Ltd. in London.

Segerstam lives near Helsinki at Tapiola with his young violinist wife, Hannele, and at the time of writing was working on his first ballet, *Pandora*, commissioned by the Finnish National Opera for production in 1967. He is now rarely heard as a performer and intends to concentrate on composition and conducting.

XXI

COMPOSERS CANNOT thrive without the additional stimulus of performance, and it is not surprising that side by side with the growth of creative musical activity we find a number of excellent performing musicians to whom is entrusted the task of creating an intelligent interest in musical appreciation, the teaching of a new generation of musicians and the propagation of works by their contemporaries.

I have already mentioned Bernhard Henrik Crusell as being one of Finland's early composers, but it must also be emphasized that he was an excellent clarinet player who started his career in a military band. That Crusell was no mean artist is illustrated by the fact that during his student days in Berlin, when money was at a low ebb, he staked everything on giving a concert which was so successful that he was able to stay in Germany and continue his very essential studies. When he went to Paris after Germany, his playing was so good that he was offered a contract with the Opéra orchestra, but he preferred to return to Scandinavia.

Although Crusell spent most of his life in Sweden—to which of course Finland was joined at that time—he gave concerts in Finland, one of which was a charity concert for the Turku Music Society in aid of the victims of a great fire at Pori. This concert was held in 1801 at a time when the society which was founded in 1790, was already well established.

But although Turku was undoubtedly the musical capital of Finland at that time, thriving music societies were also to be found in Kuopio and Oulu. These societies made it possible for soloists from Finland and elsewhere to be heard in public, and they undoubtedly stimulated the potential talent of both sexes to develop. Women traditionally had not been encouraged to take up music as a career. However, they were admitted into the Turku Music Society's orchestra as playing members in 1795, and ten years later the society sponsored a violin recital by the first Finnish woman violin soloist, Margareta Torenberg.

For nearly 100 years the Municipal Orchestra of Turku, founded in 1790, was the only permanent orchestral body in Finland. However, in 1882 the Helsinki City Symphony Orchestra came into being largely due to the perspicacity of Robert Kajanus (1856–1933) who remained conductor of the orchestra for fifty years. Kajanus was a first-class trainer and also a dynamic personality who soon won international fame. His most famous engagement was when he was invited to conduct at the World Fair in Paris in 1900 and the outside world heard the music of Sibelius for the first time. Between 1930 and 1932 Kajanus conducted several Sibelius concerts in London, and before the Second World War his Sibelius recordings were regarded as definitive. The composer and he were the greatest of friends, and there is no doubt that Kajanus was the finest interpreter of his fellow countryman's music.

Even though the outside world thought of Kajanus only in terms of Sibelius, his genius as a conductor covered the entire classical field, and his work in introducing first-class music through first-class performances in Finland is largely responsible for the very high standard of playing and appreciation throughout the country today.

After he retired from the Helsinki City Symphony Orchestra, his place was taken by another colourful conductor, Georg Schneevoigt (1872–1947), the son of a German musician from Viipuri, who also became well known in Europe, America and Australia, for his exciting orchestral virtuosity.

Quite obviously Finland could offer little hope to other conductors, and for this reason Armas Järnefelt, better known today as a composer, went to Sweden in 1907 to become principal conductor to the Royal household. Järnefelt, indeed, declared that with Kajanus in Finland there was no work for him in his home country.

The formation of other permanent orchestras throughout Finland is still continuing, even though at the moment there are now no fewer than twenty-six orchestras giving regular series of concerts. Most of these have been formed by local music societies with the assistance and encouragement of important Finnish musicians. For example, Martti Similä (1898–1958), who became permanent conductor in Helsinki in 1945, moved to Lahti in 1951 to take control of the newly created Municipal Orchestra. Similä was also a great friend and admirer of Sibelius, and was well known for his profound performances of Sibelius' Fourth Symphony.

Not surprisingly the standard of the Helsinki City Symphony Orchestra fell drastically as the result of the war, and the difficult task of bringing the orchestra back to an international level was entrusted to Tauno Hannikainen (b 1896), who is probably one of the best known Finnish musicians alive today. Together with his brothers Ilmari and Arvo, Tauno formed the Hannikainen Trio in 1919 which for fifteen years was regarded as the peak in Finnish chamber ensembles. Tauno himself, like Schneevoigt, was a cellist. Before the war, he had established himself as a symphonic conductor, but was also very highly regarded in the operatic field, particularly after conducting the premiere of Madetoja's *Pohjalaisia*. In 1941 he went to live in the USA where he soon established a considerable reputation, being invited to conduct many of the best known orchestras.

His work in Helsinki after the war cannot be too highly praised. During the twelve years of his conductorship the Helsinki City Symphony Orchestra regained its place in the international music field. Despite the fact that he retired in 1963, Hannikainen still travels widely as a guest conductor and finds time to teach a

Australian pianist Rhondda Gillespie who gave the London premiere of Usko Meriläinen's Piano Concerto, which she has also recorded for Philips. She has included modern Finnish compositions in recitals and broadcasts in Europe and Australia. *Photo; Sidney Wicebloom*

Camden Festival 1967. Heather Harper, accompanied by Walter Süsskind, in the song-cycle 'Three Leaves of Grass' by Finnish composer Leif Segerstam (texts by Walt Whitman).

Hämeenlinna Symphony Orchestra with Tauno Marttinen

younger generation in Finland both in Helsinki and Turku, where he is the head of the Institute of Music.

Another Finnish conductor, well known in the outside world, is Jussi Jalas (b 1908), who is chief conductor of the Finnish Opera as well as being professor of conducting at the Sibelius Academy. Jalas is the son-in-law of Sibelius, and all performances of the *Kullervo* Symphony since Sibelius' death have been under his direction.

Two young conductors who are certain to achieve international recognition are Jorma Panula (b 1930) and Leif Segerstam. The former has been conductor of the Helsinki City Symphony Orchestra since 1965, following studies at the Sibelius Academy with Leo Funtek and with Dean Dixon at Lund, after which he spent two years at Hilversum with Albert Wolff and Franco Ferrara. On his return from Holland in 1958 he founded the chamber orchestra of the Sibelius Academy which he still conducts, and later spent two years with the Turku Municipal Orchestra, until his Helsinki appointment which coincided with the City Orchestra's 1965 European tour.

Panula is an extremely sensitive musician. He conducts without a baton, but during the years I have watched his progress, he has created a special rapport with his orchestra so that his slightest movement is now understood and interpreted by the players. He is particularly associated with contemporary music, for which he has exceptional interpretive gifts. Finnish composers owe a great deal to him.

Segerstam has already been spoken of at length as a composer and all-round musician, so that it is only necessary in this chapter to add that he does excellent work as assistant conductor to the Opera in Helsinki and appears as guest conductor with the City Symphony Orchestra and elsewhere.

One other orchestra and their forceful conductor remain to be given special mention. This is the Radio Symphony Orchestra which has done so much work from its inception in 1927 in introducing to its large listening audience, music of all kinds with

6

special preference given to Finnish music. Toivo Haapanen (1889–1950) and Nisl-Eric Fougstedt set the high standards which have been admirably built upon by the present conductor Paavo Berglund (b 1929), who personally has made a great impression in England and elsewhere as a guest conductor. Berglund studied at the Sibelius Academy and in Vienna going on to Salzburg in 1951. He founded the Helsinki Chamber Orchestra in 1953 and was appointed assistant conductor to the Radio Symphony Orchestra in 1956, taking over the chief conductorship in 1962. In 1965 he became conductor of the Finnish Radio Chamber Orchestra and is now firmly established as one of Scandinavia's most dynamic musical personalities. Paavo Berglund directed the Radio Symphony Orchestra's first English tour in March 1967.

Obviously I have not had the opportunity of seeing and hearing every municipal orchestra in Finland, but I have been impressed by the standards in Lahti, where Urpo Pesonen, the brother of the composer, is principal conductor and also with Paavo Rautio's work in Turku and Onni Kelo's successes in the far northern town of Oulu.

XXII

FINLAND HAS produced some fine instrumental talent but it is in the operatic field that she has time and again sent out gifted musical ambassadors. The first of these was Johanna von Schoultz (1813–1863) who was a star of the Italian Opera in Paris from 1833–35, after which she spent three years singing in Italy with tremendous acclaim. She was most famous as Rosina in *The Barber of Seville*, in which Rossini himself coached her—as did Bellini, Donizetti and Auber in their operas. She shared a concert programme with Liszt, and her meteoric career was at its height when she had a haemorrhage at the age of twenty-five, the aftermath of which caused her to abandon her career. She had been called 'The Nightingale of Finland' when she was made a member of the Swedish Academy of Music at the age of eighteen and offered the then phenomenal sum of 90,000 francs per annum to join the Madrid Opera as prima donna.

Alma Fohström (1856–1936) toured the world as well as appearing under contract with the Metropolitan Opera in New York and the Imperial Opera in Moscow. Whilst in Russia, she was professor at the St Petersburg Conservatory from 1909–1918, after which she taught in Berlin until 1928.

A Finnish singer who made a great success in London at Covent Garden was Aino Ackte (1876–1944) whose Paris début in Gounod's *Faust* was nothing short of sensational. She sang in New York at the Metropolitan, as well as Covent Garden, making a tremendous impression as Salome. Upon her return to Finland in 1911, she collaborated with Edward Fazer in re-founding the Finnish Opera of which she later became director.

Richard Strauss' music seems to have attracted Finnish women singers, for Hanna Granfelt (1884–1952) was conspicuously successful at the Berlin State Opera between 1915 and 1922 as Salome and Ariadne, as well as singing Oktavian in *Der Rosenkavalier* under the baton of the composer. She also made a few early gramophone records.

Nearer to our own time is Aulikki Rautavaara (b 1906), whose performances at the 1937 Salzburg Festival and also at pre-war Glyndebourne were memorable, particularly in Mozart roles. One of her last appearances was at the Edinburgh Festival in 1949, when she sang several of Sibelius' songs with conspicuous success. Happily this fine artist made many records.

Since the death of Kirsten Flagstad, Wagnerites have been looking for a new idol as Brünnhilde and Isolde. One of the most popular at the moment is Anita Välkki (b 1926) whose appearances at Bayreuth, the Metropolitan and Covent Garden are invariably sold out. I also remember a notable *Turandot* in London in 1965.

Mariaheidi Rautavaara (b 1927) the wife of Einojuhani, won the coveted Queen Elisabeth singing competition in Brussels, after which she received invitations to many of the principal opera houses in Europe including Bayreuth. Nevertheless, she temporarily retired to bring up her young family, but I am happy to say that she is now returning to the concert and opera stages. She is especially noted for her interpretation of the songs of Yrjö Kilpinen, as well as taking the leading soprano role in her husband's opera *Kaivos*. She, too, has had success in Britain.

Raili Kostia has been a regular guest artist in Austrian and German opera houses for many years as well as having a fine reputation for lieder singing. A younger singer, Taru Valjakka, gave her first concert in 1964 and appeared as Donna Anna in Helsinki that same spring. She has studied at Salzburg under Erik Werba and with Gerald Moore in Stockholm. In August 1966 she was soloist during a concert tour of the USA by the Klemetti Institute Chamber Choir and the same year performed at the ISCM Festival in Stockholm. In 1967 she made her London début as soloist in the world première of Kokkonen's *Laudatio Domini* by the Finnish Radio Chamber Choir at their Camden Festival appearance.

Best known among the male Finnish singers is probably Kim Borg (b 1919), who has appeared on the concert platform and in opera all over the world with special successes at the Metropolitan and Glyndebourne, as well as at the Salzburg, Edinburgh and Prague Festivals. Borg is a first-class actor as well as being the possessor of a rich bass voice, and these gifts give his lieder recitals a special dramatic significance.

In 1950 Matti Lehtinen (b 1922) won the voice competition in Geneva, since when he has gained much praise for his performances of Schubert and Schumann, as well as appearing in opera in various parts of Europe. He is professor of singing at the Sibelius Academy, but this does not prevent him from making extensive tours to the USA, Canada and other parts of the world.

Martti Talvela (b 1935) is at present a member of the Deutsche Oper in West Berlin, but he too is regularly seen as a guest artist in Stockholm, Bayreuth, La Scala and elsewhere.

Another young singer who is slowly but surely making a considerable career is Tom Krause (b 1934). He has been seen in London, although most of his work is with opera companies in Germany. In common with Kari Nurmela, a Finnish baritone working primarily in Central Europe, Krause is expected to make a big career. In the instrumental field it is Finnish cello players who are making names for themselves internationally. Erkki Rautio and Arto Noras, in particular, gave memorable London débuts in 1967, and Arto Noras was the second prizewinner in the 1966 Tschaikowsky Competition in Moscow.

With enterprising young orchestras and conservatoires as well as the enthusiasm of the younger generation of performing artists, the contemporary Finnish composer is given more and more opportunity to develop. Summer festivals, notably in Jyväskylä and Savonlinna—to say nothing of the annual festivals in Helsinki—help to create publicity and occasions where Finnish music is given an airing under favourable conditions. There is even a strong hope that these may one day be co-ordinated into a Festival of Finland, which I feel would be a wonderful idea.

Whatever the future may hold, Finland is no longer culturally the poor sister of Scandinavia or indeed of Western Europe. Her musicians have confidence and pride in their achievements, as well as a national integrity and an international vision.

Appendix

ERIK BERGMAN

Op 1 Piano Trio
    2 Suite for string orchestra
    3 Passacaglia & fuga for organ
    4 Six songs (Arvid Mörne) with piano
    5 Five songs (L. Onerva & K. Sarkia)
    6 'Rakastetulle' (To the Beloved)
      (Y. Kaijärvi), song cycle
    7 Sonate concertante for piano
    8 Sonata for violin and piano
    9 Three dances for violin and piano
  10 Musica da camera for soprano, flute, violin, cello and piano
  11 *a)* Songs *b)* Arrangement for boys' choir
  12 Songs for mixed choir
  13 'Danze senza nome' for piano
  14 (Destroyed)
  15 Four songs (J. L. Runeberg)
  16 Five psalms (Book of Psalms)
  17 'Kotikylä' (Home Village) (Y. Kaijärvi)
     (Dance, Return from Work, Polkka), cycle for male choir
18–19 (Destroyed)
  20 'Majnätter' (May nights)
     (Jarl Hemmer) for soprano and orchestra
  21 Songs with piano (Gustaf Fröding)
  22 Three less serious songs I (text: Jan Fridegård)
  23 Biblical fantasias (text: Gustaf Fröding)
24–26 (Destroyed)
  27 'Ensamhetens sånger' (Songs of Solitude)
     (Edith Södergran) for voice and orchestra

P. Lagerkvist, K. Boye), four love songs for voice and
piano
46 'Tre aspetti d'una serie dodecafonica' for orchestra
47 *a)* 'Adagio' (Bo Bergman), for male choir, baritone,
flute, tremolo
b) 'Svanbild' (Solveig von Schoultz) for solo voice,
solo quartet, male choir
c) 'Nu sjunger slätterna' (Hjalmar Krokfors) for male
choir
48 'Aubade', for orchestra
49 'Aton' (Echnatons Solhymn) for baritone, reciter and
mixed choir
50 *a)* 'Psalm' (Solveig von Schoultz) for mixed choir
b) 'Junibastu' (Solveig von Schoultz) for male choir
51 *a)* 'Drei Galgenlieder' (Christian Morgenstern) for male
choir, baritone, speaking choir and two speaking voices
b) 'Vier Galgenlieder' (Christian Morgenstern) for
speaking choir and three speaking voices
52 'Simbolo' for orchestra
53 Concertino da camera, for eight soloists (flute, clarinet,
bass clarinet, percussion, piano, violin, viola, cello)
54 Bauta, for baritone, male choir, percussion (text: Eddan)
55 'Sela', for baritone, mixed choir and chamber orchestra
(text from Book of Psalms, new translation by
Martin Buber)
56 *a)* 'Fåglarna' (The Birds) (Solveig von Schoultz) for
male choir, baritone, five solo voices, percussion, celesta
b) 'Barnets dröm' (Child's dream) (Elmer Diktonius)
for a child voice (speaking), two speaking voices
(tenor and bass), recorder, male choir
57 *a)* 'Hä Li Bomp', suite for reciter, tenor, male choir
(Lars Hulden)
b) 'Tuonelas hjordar' (Harry Martinson) (Hommâge à
Jean Sibelius)
58 'Circulus', for orchestra

59 *a)* 'Snösvit' (P. Sandelin) for baritone, male choir and
flute
b) 'Springtime' (Solveig von Schoultz) for mixed choir

HENRIK OTTO DONNER

Tre Studier (Three Studies) for speech, chorus, mixed chorus and
soprano solo
Three Pieces for piano
Three Pieces for flute and piano
Cantata Profana for soprano, tenor and baritone and chamber
ensemble
Ideogramme I for clarinet, trombone, flute, percussion and
twelve radios (or tape)
Ideogramme II for twenty musicians and tape and promenade room
3 Bagateller for piano
Esther electronic (does not exist in full anymore)
For Emmy, 2 for nineteen musicians (amplifier and six micro-
phones required)
Siamfoni for trumpet, trombone and French horn (team com-
position)
'Moonspring' or 'Aufforderung Zum' . . . or Symphonie I
(Homâge à Ives) for string orchestra, guitar, harp and electronic
organ
6 Bagateller for string quartet
'To Whom It May Concern' for symphony orchestra

TOIVO ELOVAARA
Orchestral Compositions
'Juhannus-sarja' (Midsummer suite)
'Satukirja' (Story book)
'Harjoitelma orkesterille' (Study for orchestra)
Symphonic Poem
Symphonic Poem
Sinfonietta for string orchestra
Coral from Old Church Book, harp and strings

Music to play 'Viisauden jyvä' (Wisdom's Seed, fairytale)
Symphonic poem
Symphony in A minor

Chamber Music

String Quartet in C minor
Piano Trio in D major, violin, cello and piano
Prelude and Fuga in E minor, for three clarinets
Introduction and Fuga in E minor, for flute, oboe, clarinet and bassoon
Sonata for violin and piano in D minor
Largo for string quartet in C-sharp minor
String Quartet in D minor
Sonatina for two violins and cello in F minor
Sonatina for string quartet in B-flat minor
String quartet in C-sharp minor (Erkki Melartin in memoriam)
Hymn for Kantele and organ in E minor
Hymn for string quartet in C major
Sonata for piano and violin in D minor

Piano Compositions

Andante, F-sharp minor
Four Etudes
'Yö-kuvia' (Night scenes)
Prelude F-sharp minor
'Kultapilviä' (Golden clouds)
Prelude in E major
Prelude in F-sharp minor
Häämarssi (Wedding March) G-sharp major
Prelude, E minor
Satu-kuvia (Fairytale scenes)
Sonatina, in B-flat minor
Impromptu, C-sharp minor
Hymn, in F-sharp minor
Choral from Old Hymn Book
Kehto-laulu (Cradle song), F-sharp major
Häämarssi (Wedding March), A major

Impromptu, E major
Valsette, A minor
Five Impromptus
Cycle of Christmas songs for Kantele
Lasten maailmasta (From the world of children)
Passacaglia for two pianos, in B-flat minor
Vanhan Viipurin kuvia (Scenes from Old Viipuri)
Metsä-järvi (Forest lake) for piano and kantele
Ol kaunis kesä-ilta (On a beautiful summer night)
Illan hämärtyessä (At twilight)
Hymni (Häähymni) (Wedding Hymn) for piano and organ,
D major
Hymn, E major
Kuvia Bornholm'nilta (Scenes from Bornholm)
Hymn D major

Organ Compositions
Urkukoraali: Sua Jeesus Kristus kiitämme (Organ chorale: We
thank you Jesus Christ)
Prelude and fuga, E minor
Prelude, E minor
Organ chorales: Oi riemu kun saan tulla (O joy that I may come),
Jeesusta nyt Goltalle (Jesus now to Golgotha) Oi Herra ilo suuri
(O Lord great joy)
Prelude, in E-flat major
Organ Chorale: Auta, oi Jeesus (Help us, O Jesus)
Prelude, in F-sharp minor
Prelude, in E minor
Organ chorale: Veni Cretor Spiritus
Kirkkautta kohti kuljen (I go towards the glory) partita

Music for plays
Viisauden jyvä (See orchestra)
Pekka Peloton (Peter, the Fearless) by Ukko Kivistö, piano
accompaniment

Melodramas
Three melodramas, words by Edith Södergran, translated by
Uuno Kailas
Recitation and piano
1. Pohjolan kevät (Northern Spring)
2. Minä näin puun (I saw a tree)
3. Auringon noustessa (At sunrise)
Koti (Home), words by Lauri Pohjanpää. Piano accompaniment
On maa (The earth), words by Saima Harmaja. Piano accompaniment
Keväällä (In the Spring), words by Mauri Keikkala. Piano accompaniment
Äidin-laulu (Mother's song), words by Kanerva Hirvi-Kunnas.
Piano accompaniment
Kristus Getsemanessa (Christ in Gethsemane) Text from the
Bible. Piano accompaniment
Mullan-virsi (Song of the earth), words by Mauri Heikkala. Piano
accompaniment
Getsemane (Gethsemane), words Oke Peltonen. Piano accompaniment
Numerous solo songs, duets, choral compositions and arrangements and various cantatas

EINAR ENGLUND
Quintet for piano and string quartet
Symphony No. 1
Epinikia , symphonic poem for large orchestra
Symphony No. 2
Suite from the incidental music to the play 'The Great Wall of
China' for large orchestra
Sinuhe, Suite from the ballet for small orchestra
Four Dance Impressions for large orchestra
Suite from the film 'The White Reindeer' for orchestra
Cello Concerto
Piano Concerto
Incidental music to the play 'Tadd' for small orchestra

Odysseus, Suite from the ballet for large orchestra
'Introduction and Toccata' for piano
'Notturno' for piano

ERIK FORDELL
Fourteen symphonies
Five piano concertos
Eight suites for string orchestra
Two violin sonatas
Five cantatas
Various other compositions including songs, choral music and
works for piano solo

LEO HÄRKÖNEN
His earlier works were lost during the war, and the following are
his most important works:

Op 25 'Hellaan laakeri' (Laurels of Hellas)
(Aale Tynni), for mixed choir and orchestra
35 'Commedia dell'Arte', Suite for orchestra
37 'Hymni kauneudelle' (Hymn to beauty) for male choir
and orchestra
39 Symphony I (four movements)
41 'Meri aukeaa' (Tauno Koskela) for male choir and
orchestra
46 'Lyrical suite' for orchestra
47 'Tiesi tunne' (Arvi Kivimaa) for male choir and orchestra
48 'Olympic Hymn' (Pindaros), for mixed choir and
orchestra
49 Symphony II (four movements)
51 'Piae Cantiones' (V. A. Koskenniemi), cantata for choir,
soloists and orchestra
53 'Lammaspaimenten jouluyö' (Shepherds' Christmas
night) (A. Kippola), cantata for youth, organ accompaniment
54 'Dramatic Suite' for orchestra (three movements)

57 'Seitsemän pientä kiliä' (Seven small kids) musical story for recitation, vocal soloists and orchestra

58 'Autiomaa' (Desert) (Viljo Kajava), cantata for women's choir and orchestra

68 Concertino for viola and chamber orchestra

70 Divertimento for trumpet, two violins and piano (four movements)

71 'Hämeenmaa' (Uno von Schrowe 1874), cantata for male choir, soloist and piano

72 'Heinolan laulu' (A. Kippola), for male choir and piano

PAAVO JOHANNES HEININEN

Toccata for piano
'Sonatine 1957' for piano
Symphony I
Concerto for String orchestra
Preambolo for orchestra
Tripartita for orchestra
Suite for three wind instruments
Quintet for flute, saxophone, piano, vibraphone and percussion
Canto di natale (Jacopone da Todi) for soprano and piano
Petite symphonie joyeuse (Symphony II)
Music for the play 'Mariana Pineda' by Lorca
'Easter passacaglia' (Baritone solo, mixed chorus and organ) for a TV play
Soggetto per orchestra da camera
Musique d'ete for violin, saxophone, guitar and percussion
Adagio for orchestra
Piano concerto No. 1
Discantus for flauto, contralto solo
Dedicatio: F H for organ (in memoriam F. J. Heininen)
Poesia squillante ed incadescente (piano sonata)
Piano concerto No. 2

MAURI HONGISTO

Violin Concerto

Piano Concerto
Piano Trio
Prelude and Fuga for orchestra
Symphonic work for male choir and orchestra
String Quartet
Composition for female choir and orchestra
Composition for male choir and orchestra
Composition for string orchestra
Cantata for female choir and orchestra

Also:
Numerous songs for choirs, male, female and mixed choirs
Numerous solo songs for female and male voices
Numerous piano pieces
A musical fairy tale for the Finnish Broadcasting Corporation
Songs for children and piano pieces for children, etc. etc.
(unfinished orchestra compositions)

JOHANSSON, BENGT
Piano Concerto
Stabat Mater
Variations for 'cello and orchestra
The Tomb Akr Caar for baritone and chorus
Requiem
Various other works for orchestra, chorus, organ, chamber ensembles, and some electronic music

REIJO EINARI JYRKIÄINEN
Frammenti per il septetto d'archi, 3 vni, 2 vle, vc, cb

Sounds I	concret music on tape
Sounds II	concret music on tape
Idiopostic	electronic music on tape
For four	cl, perc, guitar, vn

Contradictions fl, cl, perc, guitar, string quartet

AHTI KARJALAINEN

Op 1 Polonaise for trombone solo
  2 Rondo, for violin and piano
  3 'Kevad' (Hans Kint), voice and piano
  4 Partita Nr I trumpet, corno and trombone
    Marssi vanhaan tapaan (March, traditional)
    Menuetto
    Ameriikkalainen humoreski (American humoresque)
  5 Overture in E major
  6-1 Kehtolaulu (Lullaby) (Haahtela) voice and piano
  6-2 Kuunsilta (Moon Bridge) (T. Pajunen—Kivikäs) voice and piano
  7 'Merikoski', musical poem
  8 'Asmusta iltaan' (From morning to night), country scenes, symphonic poem
  9 'Perintövala' (Ruoska) mixed choir
  10 Voimistelumusiikkia (Music for gymnastics) piano
  11 'Hakkaa päälle' Overture
  12 Scherzo, for trumpet or trombone and orchestra
  13 Partita Nr 2, trumpet, French horn and trombone (Introduction, humoresque and nocturno)
  14 1. 'Leijonamarssi' (The Lion March)
     2. 'Panssarimarssi' (The Armour March)
     3. 'Träskimarssi', piano
     4. 'Pihlajasaarimarssi', piano
  15 1. 'Suomen vartio' (Ilmari Pimiä), voice and piano
     2. 'Vapaudenmaa' (T. Pajunen-Kivikäs), voice and piano
  16 Concerto for Trombone and orchestra (Grave—Allegro ma non troppo, II Andate, III Allegro ma non troppo)
  17 a) String Quartet in C Major
       I Andante sostenuto—Allegro commodo
       II Andante sostenuto quasi cento
       III Scherzando quasi Allegro
       IV Allegro conbrio
  17 b) Andante religioso, string quartet

89

17   c) Allegro commodo, string orchestra
18   'Kesäisiä kuvia' (Summer Scenes), Suite for oboe and
     orchestra (Ia and b Aamu, II Paimentunnelma,
     III Sirkkojen hypyt, IV Niitty lepää, V Paimenpojan
     karkelo)
19   Muunnelmia Suom. sotilaslaulusta (Variations on Finnish
     Soldier's Song)
20   Sextet (I Andante quasi lento—Allegro con moto,
     II Andante sostenuto quasi lento, III Allegro Scherzando)
21   Preludio and Allegro, for violin and piano
22   1. 'Keväälle' (To the Spring) (Einari Vuorela), voice and
        piano
     2. Villilintu (Wild Bird) (T. Pajunen-Kivikäs), voice and
        piano
     3. Tyrskyt (Breakers) (T. Pajunen-Kivikäs), voice and
        piano
23   Tema con Variozioni per fl. ob. and orch.
24   'Pajolaistanssi' (Devil's Dance), violin and piano
25   Notturno, viola or cello and piano
26   'Kontrapunktisia muunnelmia ja fuuga jousiorkesterille'
     (Counterpoint Variations and Fuga for Strings) string
     orchestra
27   a) Juhlafanfaari No. 1 ja 2 (Festival Fanfare)
     b) 6 fanfaaria (6 Fanfares)
     c) Kisafanfaari No. 1, 2 ja 3 (Games fanfares)
     d) Kotkan Meripaivien fanfaari (Fanfare for Kotka's
        Sea Festival)
28   Festival Fanfare for Centenary of Finnish Railways,
     Nr 1, 2 and 3
29   'Talvikuvia' (Winter Schemes) Suite for symphony
     orchestra (I Talvipäivä, II Mäenlaskua, III Kuutamo,
     IV Jäidenlähtö)
30   Symphony No. 1 in C minor
        I Andante sostenuto—Allegro ma non troppo
        II Andante quasi larghetto

2. Sotapoikien lähtölaulu (K. Väänänen) voice and piano
3. Hissun kissun (T. Pajunen-Kivikäs) voice and piano
4. Pohjolan portti (E. Asikainen) voice and piano

40 Concerto per Violin and orchestra
  I Allegro moderato
  II Andante quasi bolero
  III Allegro energico

41 1. *(a)* and *(b)* Pyhäkoululaisten laulu, voice and piano
  2. Pääsiäinen
  3. Jouluriemua (H. Antikainen), mixed choir

42 1. Kotiseutuvirsi, voice and piano
  2. Karhulan laulu (Terttu Peltola), voice and piano

43 1. Juomalaulu (Eino Koivistoinen), male quartet and
     accordion
  2. Satamalaiturilla (E. Koivistoinen), voice and piano

44 'Elon vuo' (Ville Oksanen), female choir or voice and
     piano

45 'Sun luonas rauhan saan', female choir

46 Ostinato, for cello and piano or orchestra

47 'Kirjokannen kappaleita', Suite for Vl. Viol. ab- Engl.
     and soprano (I Kylvö, II Kasvu, III Sato)

48 Problema, violin and piano

49 'Missa siintää' (T. Pajunen-Kivikäs), female choir

50 Cello Concerto No. 1
  I Lento—Allegro moderato
  II Andante sostenuto
  III Allegro con moto

51 'Kuin laulu raikuva' (J. Savikko), Child choir, 3 tr.
     3 trombones or piano

52 'Metsän huilu' (E. Vuorela), child choir and strings or
     piano

53 'D, re, mi, fa, sol, la, si' (J. Savikko), child choir and
     strings or piano

54 1. 'Kullan nimi' (H. Jylhä), female or male choir
  2. 'Huhu' (J. Savikko), female choir

55 'Tervehdysvirsi' (Kalevala), child and mixed choir and orchestra
56 1. 'Varhaiskevät' (Rauha Kilpi), female choir
   2. 'Häär niityllä' (E. Vuorela), female choir
57 'Kolme laulua E. Vuorelan sanoihin' (Three songs to words by E. Vuorela), female choir and Clr. (I Juhannus yö, II Kesäjuhla, III Kesäyö)
58 'Keski-Suomelle' (To Central Finland), for orchestra
59 'Aino-neito' (Kalevala) (The Maid Aino), soprano, alto, female choir and orchestra
60 Music to play 'Mailman paras Manta' by O. Harni, voice and orchestra
61 Music to play 'Twelfth Night' by Shakespeare, voice and piano
62 Music to play 'Tuhkimo' (Cinderella) by Topelius, voice and piano
63 Music to play 'Avioliittoloma', voice and piano
64 Music to play 'Työmiehen vaimo', voice and piano
65 Music to play 'Hamlet' by Shakespeare
66 Music to Moliere's plays
67 Music to play 'Täällä Pohjan tähden alla'
68 'Äärettömyyteni laulu' (J. Savikko), soprano, violin solo, mixed choir and small orchestra
69 'Karjalan kunniaksi' (T. Lyy), male choir
70 'Rukous rukoilijoille' (Teuvo Pekkanen), male choir
71 Partita Nr 4 for String orchestra
   I Intrada
   II Rondo
   III Intimo
   IV Ironico
72 *a)* 'Lahdin laulajan pitoihin' (J. Savikko) and
   b) 'Kevään tuntua' for mixed choir and piano
73 *a* and *b)* Two Fanfares
74 Jyväskylän Rautatielaisten mieskuoron ry Lippulaulu (Flag Song for the male choir of Jyväskylä

railway workers), for male choir

75 'Saaahan Kalainen Karhi' (Kalevala), tenor, bass, male choir and orchestra

76 Suite for small orchestra (I Rondo, II Carillon, III Marziale)

77 Partita Nr 5 for flute, percussion and strings (I Moderato, II Andante, III Allegro)

78 'Kotkan tie', mixed choir and orchestra

79 'Ketju jenkasta polkkiin' (Cycle from jenkkas to polkkas) for string orchestra

80 Partita Nr 6 for bassoon, French horn, percussion and string orchestra
    I Andante-Allegro ma non troppo
    II Allegro moderato
    III Allegro

81 Cello Concerto No. 2

82 Cycle of humorous songs to Pekarinen's words for mixed choir, recitation and clarinet

JOONAS KOKKONEN

Trio for piano, violin and cello
Quintet for piano and strings
Four songs to poems of Uuno Kailas
Sonatine for piano
Cantata 'Ikivihreä' (Evergreen), written for a school chorus
Duo for piano and violin
'Illat' (The Evenings), song cycle
Music for strings
String Quartet No. 1
'Lintujen tuonela' (The Birds' Land of Death), suite for voice and orchestra
Symphony No. 1
Symphony No. 2
Sinfonia da camera for 12 strings
Missa a cappella

'Sammokon virsi sateen aikana' (The Frog's Hymn during the rain), for male chorus
'Opus sonorum' for orchestra
String Quartet No. 2
Laudatio Domini for soprano and mixed chorus
Four Christmas songs for children

ILKKA TANELI KUUSISTO
'Mustarastas' (Blackbird), for voice and piano
'Iltasiunaus' (Vespers), for mixed choir
'Lahden Laulu' (Song of Lahti), voice and piano
Organ composition
Two pieces for flute, clarinet and violin
Three Chinese songs, soprano, flute and piano
Two songs for ladies' choir
'Järvi Ja Virta' (Lake and River), male choir
Three Introductions for brass and organ
Two solo cantatas, soprano, oboe and organ
'Teinilaulu' (Student song), mixed choir
'Suo, Jeesus Rakkaani' (Grant, Beloved Jesus), motet for mixed choir
'Valkeneva Päivä' (Daybreak), cantata for soprano, baritone, mixed choir and organ
'Psalmi' (Psalm), voice and organ
Two organ chorals
Duo for flute and cello
Prelude for organ
'Joutukaa Sielut' (Haste, Ye Souls), motet for mixed choir
Five motets for mixed choir
'Herra Jeesus Hengelläsi' (Lord Jesus, with Thy Spirit), organ chorale
'Oi, Jeesus Auttaja' (O Jesus Saviour), motet for mixed choir
'In Memoriam' for organ
'Coelestis Aulae Nuntius' for trombone and organ
'Crucifixus' for baritone and string quartet

'Nunc Dimittis' for bass, trombone and organ
Two anthems
(a) Rejoice o young man, for mixed and brass choir
(b) As for man, his days are like grass, for mixed choir
Music for movie 'Leirikirje'
Music for Easter Sunday, four brass instruments
Cassatio for 2 clarinets and 2 horns
Intermezzo for clarinet and piano
Intervalls for flute and piano
Music for TV-movie 'Vantaanjoelta Vironniemelle'
Ritmo acustico I for organ, II tape music
Three recitatives for voice and piano
Music for ballet 'Effata' (Together with Reijo Jyrkiäinen)
Music for TV-movie 'Antti Puuhaara'
Music for TV-movie 'Finnish Church Architecture'
Music for TV-movies
'Sandskutan Katrina', 'Suomalaista lasia' and 'Kelirikko'
Jazzationes for jazz quartet and string quartet
'Sydämeni Laulu' (The Song of my Heart), for voice and chamber
orchestra
Merellinen sarja (Sea Suite), for mezzo-soprano and piano
Songs and music for several plays in theatre

HELVI LEIVISKA
Op 1   Piano Quartet
    2   Variationen und Final for Orchestra
    3   Suite antique for Piano
    4   Volkstänze for Orchestra
    5   Kleine Klavierstucke for children
    6   Four Gesange for orchestra
    7   Piano Concerto
    8   Orchestral Suite I
    9   'Psalmi aamusta', voice with piano
   10   Trippelfuge for Orchestra
   11   Orchestral Suite II

12 Kinderfantasien, solo songs with orchestra and piano
13 'Herz' I and II, songs with piano
14 Sonatina for piano
15 'Pimeän peikko' for choir and orchestra
16 Two intermezzi for orchestra
17 Two songs
18 Three songs
19 Two Fantasias for piano
20 'Litanie' for choir
21 Sonata for violin and piano
22 Two songs
23 Symphony I
24 Impromptu for orchestra
25 Capriccio for Piano
26 'Chant sans paroles' for small orchestra
27 Symphony No. II
28 'Mennyt Manner', Cantata for solos, choir and orchestra
29 'Canto Intima'
30 Sinfonia brevis

OSMO LINDEMAN

Trio for strings
Symphony I
Partita for percussion
Counterpoint for brass
Piano Concerto I
Symphony II
Piano Concerto II
Music for chamber orchestra (A subscription of Finnish Radio)
String Quartet
Music for films (two 'Jussi', Finnish equivalent of 'Oscar')

VILHO LUOLAJAN-MIKKOLA

Sonata for violin and piano
Rondo for violin and piano

Passacaglia and Fugue for organ
'Kyläkuvia' I, II, III (Village views), for violin and piano
Three pieces for cello and piano—'Chrysantheumum,
Kissankäpälä, Kihokki' (Three flowers)
Three pieces for piano—'Poutapilviä' (Fair weather), 'Sade'
(Rain), 'Halla' (Frost)
Scherzo for big orchestra
Hymn for choir and wind orchestra
Solo songs with piano accompaniment, songs for female, mixed
and male choirs, based on the Bible and Kanteletar and poems by
Einari, Vuorela, A. Hellaakoski, P. Mustapää, Yrjö Jylhä,
Anna-Maija Raittila, Eino Leino, Eino Viitasaari, F. E. Sillanpää,
Eero Lyyvuo, Eino Tikkanen, Vilho Myrsky, Ensio Kurki-
Suonio, Viljo Koljonen, Antero Kajanto

TAUNO MARTTINEN
Orchestral
Symphony I
Symphony II
Symphony III
Symphony IV
'Linnunrata' (The Milky Way)
Suite for orchestra
'Panu, Tulen Jamala' (Panu, God of Fire)

Concertos
Violin Concerto
'Rembrand' for Cello and Orchestra
Piano Concerto
'Dalai Lama', Cello Concerto

Ballet and Opera
'Päällysviitta' (Cloak) (Gogol), TV-opera
'Kihlaus' (Engagement) (A. Kivi), opera
'Tulitikkuja lainaamassa' (Borrowing matches) (Maiju Lassila),
opera

'Apotti ja Ikäneito' (Le Curé de Tours) (Balzac), opera
'Hymy tikkaiden juurella' (The Smile at the Foot of the Ladder)
(Henry Miller), opera, ballet

Kalevala Themes
'Lemminkäinen äiti' (Mother of Lemminkäinen), symphonic poem
'Kokko, ilman lintu' (Eagle, Bird of the Air), mezzo soprano and
orchestra
'Lemminkäinen äiti Tuonelan joella' (Mother of Lemminkäinen
at Tuonela River), mezzo soprano and orchestra
'Lemminkäinen lähtö Pohjolaan' (Lemminkäinen's departure to
the North), cantata for mezzo soprano, alto, baritone, bass
'Lemminkäinen Pohjolassa' (Lemminkäinen in Pohjola), cantata
for alto, baritone, bass, chorus and orchestra

Piano Compositions, etc.
Sonata I
Sonata II
5 'Mustat viitoset'
Sonata III
16 Inventions
4 Preludes
'Titisee', suite for piano
'Panu', for two pianos
'Nonetto'
'Loitsu' (Magic), for three percussionists
'Kellot' (Bells), for three percussionists

Song Cycles
'Pidot' (Feast) (Liisa Heikkerö)
'Kuoleman unia' (Dreams of Death) (Pirkko Jaakola)

Choral Works
'Gabbata' (Bible), for tenor, baritone, narrator, choir and string
orchestra

Kalevalainen sarja mieskuorolle (Kalevala Suite for male choir):
Sammon synty, Ei ilo ilolle nousnut, Väinämöisen soitto
Delta for Clarinet and piano

USKO MERILÄINEN
Orchestral Works
'Sumu' (The Mist), Symphonic Fantasia
Partita for brass
Symphony I
Concerto for orchestra
Piano Concerto
Concerto da camera, violin solo, due orch. d'archi and perc.
'Epyllion' for orchestra
Symphony II
Ballet 'Arius' (Ruokojen kulkue)

Chamber Music
Four bagatelles for string quartet
'Impression'
String Quartet
Arabesques for cello solo
Hommage à J. S. (Jean Sibelius), violin and piano
'Opusculum' (Metamorphosi for violin solo)

Piano Music
Suite for Piano
Piano Sonata I
Piano Sonata II
Sonatina for Piano
Three Nocturnes

Vocal Music
Four songs (Pekka Lounela)

Music for Plays
'Peer Gynt' (Ibsen)
'Oikeamieliset' (Camus)
'Eros and Psykhe' (Eeva-Liisa Manner)
'Viimeiset kiusaukset' (Kokkonen)

TOIMI PENTTINEN
Op 1 Etude for piano
   2 'Pilviä' (Clouds), suite for orchestra
   3 'Katukuva' (Street Scene), Fantasia for orchestra
   4 Piano Trio in B flat major
   5 Prelude and Fuga for Organ
   6 1. Romance for violin and piano
     2. Romance for violin and piano
   7 Sonata for violin and piano in G Major
   8 Three songs:
     No. 1 'Autio mökki' (Deserted cottage)
     No. 2 Suo keväällä' (Marsh in the spring)
     No. 3 'Hankiaamuna' (Snowdrift in the morning)
   9 Motet for mixed choir
  10 Rondoletto for violin and piano
  11 Four Organ Preludes
  12 Valse Caprice for violin and piano
  13 Concerto for organ and orchestra

ARVO RÄIKKÖNEN
Songs for female choir a cappella, about 20 works. In addition to these:
Cycle of Finnish folk melodies for female choir and small orchestra
Cycle of Hungarian folk melodies for female choir and piano
Cantata 'Ikikestävät aarteet' (Everlasting treasures), for female choir and piano
Cantata 'Meri edessäs aukeaa' (In front of you opens the sea), for female choir and piano

Cantata 'Elämän laulu' (The song of the Life) (Sarkia), for female choir and orchestra, first performance in Turku 1964

Songs for male choir a cappella, about 30 works. In addition to these
Cantata 'Ensimmäinen purje' (The first Sail) (Koskela), for male choir and orchestra
Cantata 'Taivaaseen käy matkamme' (Our journey leads to Heaven), for male choir and boys' choir and organ. It is based on the religious Finnish folk melodies
A few compositions a capella for the combination of male and boys' choirs

Songs for mixed choir a cappella, about 15 compositions, with special mention of Psalm 86 (Kallista Herra Korvasi)
In addition to these:
Cantata 'Pohjantähti' (Onerva), for mixed choir and orchestra
Psalm 96 (Pohjanpää) (Tulkaa Herran eteen riemulla), for mixed choir and orchestra
Veljesliekki, for mixed choir and orchestra

Songs for Children and Youth, dozens! Among them:
'Nuoret puut' (Young Tress), for children's choir and piano (Orchestra)
Ballet pantomime 'Jörö-Jukka' (Sulky) (Three poems of Hoffman's fairytales)

Solo songs, about 30 compositions. In addition to these:
Song Cycle 'Kevät, Kesä, Syksy' (Spring, Summer, Autumn) (Kouta), for soprano and orchestra

Orchestra Works
'Tanhu' (Dance), received a prize in a competition arranged by the Finnish Broadcasting Corporation.

Vesper Music
'Tammisunnuntaivesper' (January Sunday Vesper) (In memory
of the beginning of the Finnish Independence Campaign)

EINOJOHANI RAUTAVAARA

Op 1 Pelimannit
   2 Quartettino—String Quartet I
   3 A Requiem in Our Time
   4 Table-Music for Duke John
   5 Symphony I
   6 Icons—Suite for piano
   7 Seven Preludes
   8 Symphony II
   9 Fünf Sonette an Orpheus (poems R. M. Rilke), for voice
     and piano or voice and orchestra
  10 Ludus Verbalis
  11 Oboe Quartet
  12 String Quartet II
  13 Die Liebenden, for voice and orchestra
     (Poems: R. J. Rilke)
  14 Drei Sonette an Orpheus, for voice and piano
     (R. M. Rilke)
  15 Kaivos (The Mine), opera
  16 Canto, for string orchestra
  17 Overture to 'Kaivos'
  18 String Quartet III
  19 Missa duodecanonica, for chorus
  20 Symphony III
  21 Songs to poems of Bo Setterlind
  22 Nattvarden, for mixed chorus (Poems: Bo Setterlind)
  23 Syksy virran suussa, for male choir (Poem: Toivo
     Pekkanen)
  24 Arabescata, for orchestra
  25 Symphony IV
  26 Sonata for bassoon and piano

27 Lu/ut for mixed chorus (Poems from the Kalevala)
   Three Sonnets of Shakespeare
   Laulaja, for male chorus (from Kalevala)
   Ave Maria
   Three religious songs

MATTI RAUTIO
Suite for Piano
'Sininen haikara' (The Blue Stork), miniature ballet
Divertimento for Cello and Orchestra
Piano Concerto
and a great number of small compositions for music pedagogical
purposes, e.g. 'Iloinen soittoniekka', fifty small piano pieces
'Pikku Peimlannit' folksongs, for two violins

NILS-ERIC RINGBOM
Andantino grazioso for piano
Andante interrotto for violin and piano
Romanza for viola and piano
Tema con variazioni for piano
Pieni sarja (Little suite)
Musica di concerto for violin solo and orchestra
Andantino for violin and piano
Till livet (To Life) (Erik Therman)
Two songs (Erik Therman):
Liten visa
Steg en gud ur det hoga
Funebre for organ
Symphony No. 1
Two songs (Edith Södergran), for mixed choir:
O himmelska klarbet
Sommar i bergen
Vandrerska (Wanderer), three songs for soprano and orchestra
Symphony No. II
Ur en dagbok (From a Diary) (K. G. Hildebrand), for soprano
and piano

Duo for violin and viola
Four songs (Gunnar Björling), for mezzo soprano and orchestra
Symphony No. III
Hymn to Helsingfors (Rabbe Enckell), for mixed choir and
orchestra
Quartetto per archi
Sestetto
Symphony No. IV

LAURI SAIKKOLA

String Quartet I in G minor
Double Canzonet for string quartet and piano
'1500 metriä' (1500 Metre Race), parody for orchestra
'Huhtikuu' (Vuorela), 'Varjoleikki' (Vuorela), for male choir
Solo songs:
'Rannalla' (Harmaja), string orchestra or piano acc.
'Aamu' (Harmaja) with piano
'Partita', Orchestra Suite
'Pastorale', Orchestra Suite
'Quartetto burlesco', string quartet
Sonatini in C Major for piano
Trio for flute, viola and contra bassoon
Suite for contra bassoon and piano
Sinfonia campale I
'Joukahaisen kosto' (Joukahainen's Revenge) (Kalevala), for male
choir, tenor and orchestra
'Sairas', song cycle to words by Saima Harmaja
'Kuvia Karjalasta' (Scenes from Karelia), orchestra suite
'Karjala palaa' (Karelia in Flames), symphonic picture for
orchestra
Nocturne for cello and orchestra
Solo songs to words by Saima Harmaja
Sinfonia tragica (II)
For string orchestra:
Pieni elegia (Little elegy), Ajatelma (Aphorism), Pieni sävelmä
(Little melody)

'Rantakalmisto Vepsässä', song for male choir
'Serenata' for string orchestra (Prelude, Minuet, Fuga, Adagio, Rondo)
Canzona for string orchestra
Symphony III
Overtura dell' dramma
Sonatina for violin and piano (Prologo, Intermezzo, Canone, Epilogo)
Sonatina for viola and piano
Musica per archi
'Taivaaseen menijä' (Going to Heaven), folk story for speaker, soloists, choir and orchestra
Symphony IV
Miniature compositions for piano:
Sentimento, Giocoso, Fuga, Marcia, Interludio, Nocturno
Concerto for violin and orchestra
Divertimento for five wind instruments
Concerto for cello and chamber orchestra
Arioso for cello and piano
Concerto di camera for piano and chamber orchestra
Suite for clarinet and piano (miniature composition):
Preludi, Staccato, Legato, Burla
'Ristin', opera (Lauri Haarla)
Symphony V
Finnish Television's signature tune
Grave for trombone and organ
Pezzi per archi: Primo, Secondo, Terzo, Quarto, Epilogo
Musica sinfonica

AULIS SALLINEN
Two mythical scenes for orchestra
String Quartet I
Concerto for Chamber Orchestra
String Quartet II (Canzona)
Variations for Violoncello and Orchestra

Three lyric songs of Death, for baritone, male choir and chamber
orchestra
Mauermusik, for orchestra
14 Juventas Variations, for orchestra
Serenade for two Wind Quartets
Elegy to Sebastian Knight for cello and orchestra
Metamorphosis for piano and chamber orchestra
Quattro per Quattro
Cadenze per violino
Nocturne for Piano

ERKKI SALMENHAARA

Sonata for cello and piano
Trio for violin, viola and cello
'Nove improvvisazione', concerto for piano, string orchestra and
timpani
'... la clarté vibrante ...', Cantata for soprano, four celli and
percussion (text: Baudelaire)
'Suoni successivi' for grand piano and two players
'Crescendi' (Symphony I) for orchestra
'Pan and echo' for four piatti sospesi, tam-tam and amplifier
Composizione per quartetto d'archi
Concert for two solo violins with amplifiers
'White label' (Electronic music)
Symphony II for orchestra
Composition 3 for violin, clarinet, guitar and percussion
Elegie I for three Flauti, two Trombe and Contrbass
Elegie II for two String Quartets
Chaconne for orchestra
Cantullus amans. Three songs for male chorus (text in Latin:
Catullus)
'Kuun kasvot' (The Face of the Moon), four songs for mixed
chorus (text (Finnish): Pentti Saarikoski)
Siam Phony. A part of a collective composition for brass instru-
ments

Quintet for Wind Instruments
'Lenore'. A song cycle for voice and piano (text (Finnish): Anja Kosonen)
Three French songs for voice and piano (texts (English): Takahashi, Miki, Yamamura)
Symphony III for orchestra
Le Bateau Ivre, for sixteen instruments or for chamber orchestra
Toccata for organ
Elegie III for violoncello solo
Sonata for piano in E-flat Minor, with Finale in D-flat major

SULO SALONEN

4 'Aftonkantat' (Evening cantata), for mixed choir and organ
8 'Passionskantat' (Passion cantata), for mixed choir and strings
20 'Adventsmusik' for mixed choir and organ
27 'Missa a cappella'
31 'Viisauden ylistys', cantata for soloists, female choir, two violins and cello with organ
32 Requiem, for solo choir and orchestra

For Organ

7 'Variationer och fuga' (variations and fuga) (Finnish hymn)
11 Passacaglia
Zwei Partiten über Finnischen geistlichen Volkslieden 'Nyt vielä etehesi', 'Sen suven suloisuutta'
15 Partita över en finsk koral 'Taivaaseen käy matkamme'
20 Evangelical motets for choir
22 Evangelical motets
24 Toccata for organ
25 Quintet for winds
34 Partita from hymn 'Lapuan Taisteluvirsi'
'Avaja porttis, ovesi', organ prelude for High Mass

LEIF SEGERSTAM
Legend for string orchestra
Three songs to texts by Peter Sandelin
Divertimento for string quartet
Divertimento for string orchestra (revision of the above)
Five pedagogic violin duets for the violin school
Morgonen, for mixed chorus
Missa Piccola for three voices a capella or chamber chorus
Three sketches for Piano
Three 'American' songs: Lodged, A Minah Bird, A Song of the
Degrees
String Quartet No. 2
Improvisandum for unaccompained violin
Two songs for female chorus (text: Gunilla Josefsson)
Three songs to text by Viola Renwall
Three sketches for two violins
String Quartet No. 3
'Myriasm', for two violins
Three meditations for piano
Poeme for Violin and Piano
Nocturne for Piano
'Leaves of Grass', three songs for soprano, to texts from
Walt Whitman: 'Twilight', Last Lingering Drops', 'An ended
day'
Orchestral piece 'Ekvilibristicum'
String Quartet No. 4
Three songs to text by Gunnar Bjorling for soprano and piano
Ballet 'Pandora'

ERRO SIPILÄ
Fugue and Chaconne for Organ
String Trio
Partita for Wind Quintet

Two Choral Motets for mixed choir
Motets: 'Super flumina Babylonis' and 'Miserere'
Piano Sonata
Partita for Organ 'Nun komm, der Heiden Heiland'
Prelude and Fugue
Five Organ Chorales
Ten Small Organ Chorales

MARTTI TURUNEN
Vocal Works

Anssin Jukan laulu (Anssin Jukka's Song) (Folk song)
Eikä me ella veljeksiä (We're not Brothers) (Folk song)
En tiedä muistatko mua (I wonder, do you remember me ever)
(Viljo Kojo)
Eron hetkellä (At Parting)
Hanssin Jukan laulu (Hanssin Jukka's Song) (Folk Song)
Heippatirallaa (Folk song)
Hurras nyt komppania (Hurrah, Our Company) (Folk song)
Ikkunat auki aamun tuuleen (Open Windows to Morning Breeze)
(Elina Vaara)
Iltahartaus (Evening Prayer) (Einari Vuorela)
Iltalaulu (Evening song) (Folk song)
Iltapilviä (Evening Clouds) (Einari Vuorela)
Jeulu-Weinhacht (Christmas) (Carl Schauwecker)
Jouluna-Me käymme Joulun viettohon (It is now Christmas time)
(Mauno Isola)
Kaksipa tähtëä taivahalla (Two Stars in the Sky) (Folk song)
Kansa korpien (Backwoods People) (Antero Kajanto)
Karjalan kunnailla (On the Hills of Karelia) (Folk song)
Kenttien kehto (Cradles in the Battle Fields) (Unto Kupiainen)
Kesän omni (Summer Happiness)
Kirjekyyhkynen (Carrier Pigeon) (Einari Vuorela)
Kuu paistaa (The Moon Shines) (Ilmari Pimiä)
Maljalaulu (Drinking Song) (Folk song)
Matalan torpan balladi (Ballad of the Low Cabin) (Folk song)

Niin kauniisti kuin ne linnut laulaa (The Birds Sing so Beautifully)
(Folk song)
Niin kukkivat ruusut (The Roses are Blooming) (Erkki Uotila)
Niin minä neitonen (Maiden, I sing to you) (Folk song)
Nyt soikaa helkkyen (Sleigh Bells Ring)
Onnellinen aamu (Happy Morning) (Ilmari Pimiä)
Orpepojan laulu (Orphan Boy)
Pesä (The Nest) (Einari Vuorela)
Pohjola Bertel (Northern Country) (Bertel Gripenberg)
Prinsessa ja trubaduuri (Princess and the Troubadour)
(Einari Vuorela)
Pääskyläinen (The Swallow)
Rakkauden tuli palaa (Love's Flame Burns Brightly) (Folk song)
Rauhan rukous (Prayer for Peace) (Annie Besant)
Siunaus (Blessing) (Einari Vuorela)
Soi enkel laulu helkkyen (The Song of Angels Rings)
Sunnuntai (Sunday) (Aleksis Kivi)
Suomalainen rukous (Finnish Prayer) (Arvi Kivimaa)
Varjoni (My Shadow) (Yrjö Jylhä)

Songs for Choirs
Ah, kirkkaita päiviä (Ah, Bright Days), for mixed choir
(Ilmari Pimiä)
Ah, kuinka kauniilta kuuluupi (Ah, How Beautiful it sounds),
folk song for male choir
Balladi (Ballad), for female choir (Elina Vaara)
Iltalaulu (Evening Song), folk song for male choir
Jouluna (Christmas), for female, male and mixed choirs
(Mauno Isola)
Kadonnut venhe (Boat Astray), for male and mixed choir
(Einari Vuorela)
Kaipuu (Longing), for mixed choir (Severi Nuormaa)
Kaipaus (Yearning), for mixed choir (Einari Vuorela)
Kannas (Karelian Isthmus) (Ilmari Pimiä)
Kanteleeni (My 'Kantele'), for male and mixed choirs
(Kr. Haapasalo)

Karjalan kunnailla (On the Hills of Karelia), for male choir
Kenttien kehte (Cradles in the Battle Fields), for male choir
(Unto Kupiainen)
Kirkas kuu (Bright Moon), folk song for male choir
Kotimaani ompi Suomi (My Country, it is Finland), for mixed
choir
Kotini (My Home) (K. Raitie), for mixed choir
Kuu paistaa (The Moon Shines), for male choir (Ilmari Pimiä)
Laulajan laulu (The Singer's Song), for female choir (Eino Leino)
Laulu kotiseudulle (Song to my Home Country), for mixed choir
(Ilmari Pimiä)
Meidän laulumme (Our song), for female choir
Nyt lähteä mun täytyy (I must go now), folk song for male choir
Pienellä huilulla huutelem (I Play on a little flute), for mixed choir
(Einari Vuorela)
Pyhä muistojen maa (Land of Memories), for male choir
(Niilo Sauranen)
Serenada (Serenade), for male choir (R. R. Ryynänen)
Suomalainen rukous (Finnish Prayer), for mixed choir
(Arvi Kivimaa)
Suvirinteellä (On a Summer Slope), for mixed choir (I. Pimiä)
Synnyinseutu (Native Land), for female choir (I. Pimiä)
Vaeltaja (The Wanderer), for male choir (Yrjö Jylhä)

KALERVO TUUKKANEN

Op 1   Overture to the Comedy 'Lumberjacks' (Tukkijoella)
by Teuvo Pakkala, for small orchestra
2   The Tale of the Pallid Maiden (Kalvean immen tarina)
by Aleksis Kivi, symphonic poem for orchestra
3   Three songs for solo voice and orchestra
4   Serenata giocosa, symphonic suite in four movements for
orchestra
5   Three songs for solo voice and orchestra
6   Symphonic Fantasy in three movements for orchestra
7   Little Summer Suite, for small orchestra

8   Romantic Moments (Romanttisia tuokiokuvia), for strings
9   Evening Suite (Ehtoosarja), for orchestra
10 Miniatures of Chivalry (Pienoiskuvia ritarielämästä), for orchestra
11 Small Legends, for orchestra
12 Youth Suite, for orchestra
13 Religious compositions
14 Character Scenes from The Three Musketeers (Luonnekuvia Kolmesta muskettisoturista) for orchestra
15 Courtship Suite (Kosiosarja) for orchestra
16 Wanderer in the Night (Yöllinen vaeltaja) for orchestra
17 Two Marches, for orchestra
18 Legend of the Book (Kirjan virsi) by Lauri Pohjanpää, festive composition in six movements for soprano, reciter, male and boys' choir and orchestra for the 300th anniversary of Finnish printing
19 Incidental music to the play 'The Love' by Kaj Munk for strings, two flutes, two clarinets and piano
20 Concerto I for violin and orchestra
21 The Rising of the Gray Tribe (Harmaan heimon nousu), by Hokkanen, cantata for mixed choir and orchestra
22 Two Nocturnes for orchestra
23 Patriotic Suite, for male and boys' choir and orchestra
24 Symphony I for orchestra
25 Incidental music to the play 'The Golden Cranberry' (Kultinen karpalo) by Annikki Kivi, for voice, strings, harp and kantele (Ad lib. piano)
26 Songs for female choir
27 Concerto for cello and orchestra
28 Songs for mixed choir
29 A Love Song Suite (Lemmenlaulusarja) text by Einari Vuorela for solo voice (also for female choir) and small orchestra
30 Songs for solo voice and piano
31 The Bear Hunt (Karhunpyynti), text by Aleksis Kivi,

symphonic poem for male choir and orchestra

32 Vision on the Heath from the play 'The Cloud' by Helvi Hämäläinen, for orchestra
Little Suite for strings from the same play

33 Sinfonietta for mixed choir and orchestra
(text: Aale Tynni)

34 Symphony II for orchestra

35 Man and the Elements, poem in five movements for soprano, baritone, male (or mixed) choir and orchestra
(text by Yrjö Jylhä)

36 Symphony III, for soprano, tenor, mixed choir and orchestra

37 Incidental music to the play 'Moon Blind' (Kuunsokea) by Helvi Hämäläinen, for orchestra and solo voice

38 Songs for mixed choir

39 Hellenic Festive Music, for orchestra

40 The Song of the Highlands (Vuorten laulu), for orchestra

41 Christmas Suite from the play 'The Last Shepherd' by Walter Bauer, for small orchestra

42 Music to the play 'Sakuntala' by Kalidasa for woodwind, harp, percussion and solo voice

43 Songs for male choir

44 Songs for female choir

45 Concerto II for violin and orchestra

46 Songs for mixed choir

47 Incidental music to the play 'The Son of the Slave' by Jorma Eerala, for orchestra

48 The Minstrel (Runolaulaja), symphonic poem for orchestra

49 Canzonetta and Humoresque for violin and orchestra (or piano)

50 Incidental music to the play 'Amphytrion' by Moliere, for woodwind, harp, and piano

51 Incidental music to the play 'The Song of Njiilik' by Salme Härkönen, for woodwind and voice

52 Symphony IV for orchestra
53 Tempus festum, for strings
54 Symphony V for orchestra
55 Indumati, one-act opera for soprano, alto, tenor, baritone, bass and orchestra

BENGT VON TÖRNE
Symphony I
Symphony II
Symphony III
Symphony IV
Symphony V
Symphony VI
Sinfoniettas I for Mozart orchestra
Sinfonietta II for Mozart orchestra
Sinfonietta III for Mozart orchestra
10 Symphonic poems, among them: Ballad, Resurrexit,
Praeludium
Concerto for piano and orchestra
A series of chamber music works including two Sonatas for violin
and piano

Index